Studies in Jazz Discography I

Institute of Jazz Studies
University Extension Division
Rutgers University • The State University of New Jersey

Studies in

Jazz Discography I

Institute of Jazz Studies
University Extension Division
Rutgers University • The State University of New Jersey
November 1971

Price: $3.25

TABLE OF CONTENTS

SECTION I. CONFERENCE ON DISCOGRAPHICAL RESEARCH

SECTION II. SECOND ANNUAL CONFERENCE ON DISCOGRAPHICAL RESEARCH

SECTION III. CONFERENCE ON PRESERVATION AND EXTENSION OF THE JAZZ HERITAGE

FOREWORD

This series of conferences was suggested to the Institute of Jazz Studies with the objective of bringing together those people who have delved into the recording and playing careers of various jazz musicians, and who are conversant with the background of jazz as a music, with the histories of the recording companies and their products, and with other historical aspects of this general subject. It is worthy of note that essentially all of this historical and discographical research has been done by private individuals, on their own time and on the basis of their own interests, without foundation grants or outside support. These researchers are "amateurs" in the best, classic sense of the word.

Representatives of all known jazz and folk music archives, and of all music faculties within a reasonable distance of Rutgers, as well as private researchers and collectors were specifically invited to attend. I had hoped that the universities in particular would have sent representatives. We could have shown them what outstanding research has already been done by these private historians, and thereby made these faculties of music, history, and other disciplines aware of the types of theses that could be produced with jazz as a theme.

The archivists have naturally supported these conferences enthusiastically, to our mutual advantage. However, I regret that university people in the departments which could benefit the most have, with a few notable exceptions, failed to respond. I hope that these proceedings will eventually help to correct this situation, and that Institute-University cooperation will burgeon.

WALTER C. ALLEN, *Rutgers University*

INTRODUCTION

William M. Weinberg
Assistant to the President, Rutgers University
Chairman, Advisory Committee for Rutgers Institute of Jazz Studies

This volume represents the edited proceedings of the first two Annual Conferences on Discographical Research in June of 1968 and 1969 and the special conference on Preservation and Extension of the Jazz Heritage in July 1969.

The major points in each paper have been retained without any attempt to update the author's remarks. For the sake of conciseness, the editors have eliminated duplications inherent in oral presentations, particularly in panels, as well as material which depends upon its spoken context (for example, detailed discussion of musical examples). To preserve valuable audience contributions, some clarifications in response to questions have been inserted into the appropriate places in the papers; in other cases, summations of open discussions have been prepared from taped records of the meetings. Full tapes of these events are in the Archives of the Institute of Jazz Studies.

I would like to give you some background material on the Institute of Jazz Studies, and its current activities and projects

The Institute of Jazz Studies was started in the early 1950s by Marshall Stearns, with the assistance of many other jazz enthusiasts. They invested a great deal of time and energy in developing a collection of 25,000 records and almost everything that had been published about jazz up into the early 1960s.

In 1965 it occurred to some of us at Rutgers that jazz has a vital role to play within a university environment, and after meeting with John Wilson we decided to approach the Institute of Jazz Studies and consider working to gether We met with Marshall Stearns, Mrs. Jean Stearns, Sheldon Harris,

John Hammond, Eugene Kline, Robert Reisner, and others. It was obvious that the executive officers of the Institute believed that eventually the collection, to be maintained, had to be institutionalized in some way. It was agreed that the Institute of Jazz Studies be transferred to Rutgers from Waverly Place in Greenwich Village, where it was then located.

Certain conditions were established. First, the Institute of Jazz Studies was permitted to continue its growth parallel to developments in the various styles of jazz. It was to have an existence and identity of its own as a separate entity, not as a part of existing music departments or areas of academic studies. These stipulations were made because in most music departments in the United States jazz does not have the status of other forms of indigenous music. Therefore, the Institute of Jazz Studies has an autonomous status within the University. I must point out, however, that there are members of music and other departments at Rutgers who are interested in jazz and who have worked with us cooperatively.

The second condition was that the University would maintain it, store it safely, and encourage its growth. We do not intend to keep the Institute as a fixed collection; our goal is completeness and we hope that eventually it will broaden into various areas related to jazz.

The third condition was that the material in the collection be accessible. This was the most formidable problem, but it is being achieved gradually. With the presence of full-time staff members, regular procedures now exist for the use of the archives by teachers, students, and specialists. Our goal is to produce programmed materials to meet the interests of ever broader publics.

The collection found a temporary home at the John Cotton Dana Library on the Rutgers-Newark campus, pending the availability of more adequate space elsewhere.

Staff development has been encouraging. Mr. Charles A. Nanry has served as administrator on a part-time basis consistent with his faculty duties in the Department of Sociology, University College.

As full-time staff, we have the services of Mrs. Mary Prioli as assistant administrator and Richard Seidel as assistant curator. In earlier years, valuable part-time curatorial services were rendered by Vladimir Simosko.

We have had the generous assistance of devoted consultants, volunteers, and friends. At the risk of omitting some of them, let me list the following persons and their major (but not sole) areas of service: Frederic and Amelia Ramsey on research, acquisitions, curatorial problems, and visual resources; Dr. Walter Allen of the Rutgers College of Engineering and Mrs. Ann Allen on discography and research; Thomas Spence on cataloguing and acquisitions; Rudi Blesh on oral history (he has completed an ambitious project of taped interviews with the legendary Eubie Blake); Ernest Smith on film; and Donald Byrd, musician-in-residence in 1967-68.

Julius Bloom, who is Director of Concerts and Lectures at Rutgers and also Director of Carnegie Hall, has stimulated an ambitious program of live presentations totaling approximately one hundred events since 1966. George Wein has been most helpful in these programs, which have ranged from the "Jazz — The Personal Dimension" series of chamber concerts, through large-scale concerts at Carnegie Hall, to festival events at Expo '67, and in the Rutgers Stadium. Friends of the Institute, led by Jack Stine and Lee Goodman, have themselves organized annual Pee Wee Russell Memorial Stomps to provide a scholarship in the late clarinetist's name.

Jazz courses have emerged on various Rutgers campuses. The Institute has been most directly involved with those given in Newark by Christopher White, jazz bassist and fine teacher, and those in Camden by the noted critic Martin Williams.

Other conferences are on our agenda. Dr. Nanry organized a one-day meeting on "Jazz and All That Sociology" in November 1970 to survey aspects of jazz research in the social sciences; it will be published in the fall of 1971 as a *Trans-action* book.

The importance of jazz in the community has been a major interest of the Institute. While major programs await the development of special materials, there have been Jazz Week programs in the Newark schools and at Livingston College of Rutgers, under grants respectively from the Sears-Roebuck Foundation and the New Jersey State Council on the Arts. These have been administered by the Rutgers Bureau of Community Services, University Extension Division, which has provided the Institute a sympathetic administrative environment at Rutgers. David Cayer of the Bureau has developed these and other programs, has written a number of proposals for future projects, and has been responsible for fiscal management.

Our full-time staff has greatly stimulated the acquisition of new materials, but these had always continued on a significant scale through the generosity of the families of George Hoefer and Charles Edward Smith, and of Robert Reisner, Douglas Wood, Nat Hentoff, Orrin Keepnews, John Miller, and a number of others.

Our most pressing need is the development of a computerized cataloguing system which will incorporate the existing collection and new acquisitions, and eventually permit the development of an inter-institutional information system with cooperating collections throughout the nation.

In all these endeavors, the help of our friends is essential. Those who have attended these conferences on discography have earned our gratitude for their interest and support.

June 15, 1968

SECTION I

First Annual Conference on Discographical Research

WHAT IS DISCOGRAPHY: ITS GOALS AND METHODS?

D. Russell Connor
Assistant Secretary
Federal Reserve Bank of Philadelphia

The American Heritage Dictionary of the English Language defines discography as: "A catalogue of phonograph records; especially, a comprehensive list of the recordings made by a particular performer or of a particular composer's work."

That definition embraces non-musical recordings. Our interest, however, is in recorded music, and that will be my meaning when I speak of discography. I am going to speak generally about the direction discography can take and problems related to that direction, and in so doing will touch on my stated topic.

There are several kinds of discographies. There are general discographies which encompass all material in a given category — all jazz records, for instance. There are specialized discographies limited to the recorded work of a single musician or to a single period or style, such as blues. Finally, there are discographies devoted to a single artist and which include biographical date about him.

Early discographies, Delaunay's for example,[1] were of the first kind. The general discography is still in vogue — witness Brian Rust's discographies[2] covering the jazz universe, broken into time periods for convenience. Stemming from the general discographies are the more selective kinds; those reserved for a single artist, such as several about Duke Ellington,[3] or devoted to a particular genre of recorded material like the V-Disc discography.[4] The general and selective discographies, together, gave rise to the bio-discography, such as Howard Waters' Teagarden discography[5] or my own on Benny Goodman.[6]

Each type of discography has made its contribution but I would think the future of discographies lies more in the development of selective discographies, and, most likely, in the combined bio-discography. One reason is that once a general discography has been published, it is, if well done and inclusive, almost finite in nature. True, as later knowledge comes to hand, the general discography can be amended. But this can be done in the form of a supplement, or annual pamphlets to update it. My point is that the general discography need not be completely re-written and published anew, in its entirety, every five or ten years.

A second argument for the specialized discography is that it is the practical way to satisfy demands for more intense examination of a particular sector of recorded material. Sheer bulk and prohibitive cost rule out inclusion of in-depth specialization and biographical material in general discographies. The general discography can be considered a primer to survey the entire field; the specialized discography can be considered the advanced text for the specific field of inquiry.

There is, of course, a practical argument against the specialized discography; its readership is more limited. This means fewer sales, and thus a less attractive product for the potential publisher. Certainly no one interested solely in blues records, for example, would be a good prospect for a discography devoted solely to Tommy Dorsey. On the other hand a bio-discography on T.D. might attract a casual reader who couldn't care less about some obscure side Dorsey cut with Ben Selvin in 1931, but who might be interested in the full career of the personality, Tommy Dorsey. I don't think these contradictory considerations balance out; the specialized discography will sell fewer copies. But the gap between the two will narrow in the future.

If it is agreed that specialization permits intensification, then it follows that the specialized discography can and should include classes of recorded material omitted or ignored by the general discography. For example, the specialized discography can include, when appropriate, electrical transcriptions. These are not intended for public sale, but nevertheless get into the public's hands. Electrical transcriptions, invariably, are missing in general discographies, and I find this omission disturbing. Consider the great numbers of transcriptions recorded by Duke Ellington for commercial transcription companies, for government agencies, for charities, and so on. And think too of the quality of this material, both as to content and such meaningful things to the collector as surface, etc. To fail to list this category of Ellington's recorded work makes as little sense to me as ignoring Shakespeare's sonnets in a catalog purporting to be a full listing of the Bard's works.

Discographers — and collectors, too — tend to draw distinctions based on different physical properties, among other things, of recorded material. One example is the distinction between pressings and acetates, or "dubs." Another is between publicly-sold recordings and unissued material in the form of one-sided test pressings. A third is commercially-recorded versus non-commerically-recorded material. And so on, including hybrids of those I've mentioned.

I'd like to give you my views on one of these distinctions, that of commercially-recorded material as opposed to non-commercially-recorded material. This latter class includes what are known as "air checks."

I know of no discography on the market today that includes air checks. I think specialized discographies should include them. An important reason is that air checks can bridge hiatuses between commercial recording sessions, and give us a continuous record of the product of the artist. You will remember the "record ban" that began in mid-1942. For more than two years no commercial recordings were made. Did the artists quit performing between July 1942 and September 1944? Certainly not. But were it not for the amateurs who turned on their disc recorders during that time, we'd have nothing to listen to. And if you consult today's standard discographies, you would *not* find evidence of the existence of anything from those years to collect and enjoy.

That period, the record ban, is of course an extreme example. However, many of the artists with whom I am familiar have had personal gaps in their commercial recording careers. The interruptions were caused by various conditions — illness, a change in contract, tours out of the country, whatever. At times during these absences from the studios significant changes took place. Personnel shifted, instrumentation changed. Some selections were performed that never were recorded in the studios. Some selections were performed much differently than they were recorded in the studios — extended versions beyond the confines of a three-minute recording were commonplace. At times the stimulus of a "live" audience encouraged the artists to produce better versions of selections which vary also from those recorded commercially — witness Benny Goodman's Carnegie Hall concert and the Columbia and MGM albums of his off-the-air material. And a new practice is becoming important to the discographer — the fact that air checks are being "bootlegged" into pressings: for example the FDC album of Armstrong off-the-air performances.

The discographer should strive for totality, completeness, definitiveness, call it what you will. I think he does so, within the limits he sets for himself. I suggest he should enlarge these predetermined limits to include electrical transcriptions, air checks, movie soundtracks, unissued material, privately-recorded concerts, and other performances. In short, I suggest that the discographer should attempt to put on paper the whole range of "recorded" work, whether done in or out of commerical studios, whether preserved by professionals or amateurs. Certainly, in the text, he should identify each clearly; but he should consider everything, and list it all.

It goes without saying that if the discographer pursues the course I recommend he immediately vitiates this goal of totality. No one of us, nor group of us, can be assured of definitiveness once we open our work to the inclusion of electrical transcriptions, air checks, and so on. That is impossible. But just look at what *is* realized — a greatly widened picture of the *performing* life of an artist, as contrasted to the narrower view of the *commercial-recording* life of the artist. I suggest that this achievement is worth the price of falling short of totality.

One more thought on this theme: commercial recordings of the past are finite. As far as I know, the air checks of the past may be infinite; certainly we learn of new ones all the time, and this to me is the province of tomorrow's collectors. As ownership of tape recorders continues to spread, collectors will become more and more involved in making, acquiring, selling, and trading non-commerical recordings. I believe discographers had better take cognizance of this and face the future realistically.

I would like to make a few observations on the subject of methods of discography; the technique used by a discographer to compile his work. Existing discographies, written records of recording companies, trade publications, the general press, biographies, autobiographies, personal diaries, and statements of artists and collectors are all grist for the discographer's mill. And each can be an excellent source of information. However, I sometimes think in our research we ignore an obvious source of information — the recordings themselves.

I suggest that recordings must be considered a prime source, not a secondary source, of information. I know of cases in which recording sheets, and artists, have been proved wrong by the recordings. And so it goes for any source; we can find examples of recordings telling us something different from the other source.

I readily admit that recordings cannot be used as the sole authority for a discographical listing; this seems especially true in the identification of personnel. But, I insist that they cannot be ignored as a source of information. True, no author of a general discography can be expected to have examined all the recordings he lists, but I think he should state, in his foreword, what his sources are, and what they are not.

The author of a specialized discography, however, should be held to closer account. He is representing himself as an expert in a limited field. I think he can only cite particular and isolated instances where he has not been able to examine specific recordings. I don't think he is entitled to claim a blanket exemption. On the contrary, I believe the reader of the specialized discography is entitled to the blanket assumption that the author personally has examined every recording he lists, save for identified exceptions.

I was also asked to speak about some of the goals of discography. Let me name the *sine qua non* of discography — publication. Without publication there is nothing — nothing for the discographer, the collector, the librarian, or the general public. The countless hours and dollars the discographer spends come to nought if the knowledge he assembles is not shared.

Publication is the discographer's major problem. Publishers have learned that discographies have a limited sale, and can lose rather than make money. Alternatively, the publisher always has the choice of using his equipment, time, and money to publish something with a better chance of earning a profit. Nor can the publisher be faulted for this; his is not a public service enterprise, but a business whose first purpose is to make a profit.

When confronted with this reality, the discographer can undertake publication himself. I have done this, and I tell you that this is unrewarding. The expense involved, the myriad problems presented, the lack of expertise in advertising and distribution, all combine to bury the discographer-publisher. It seems unfair to ask the discographer to take on the job of publication and, in any event, it doesn't work well.

I've long thought that one answer to this problem lies in subsidization. I believe that the discographer's work is relatively as important as many of the projects subsidized by funds, by institutions, and even by agencies of the government. The Ford Foundation would not waste money by underwriting publication of works on jazz music, which is America's only unadulterated contribution to world culture. Institutions like Rutgers can justify use of its press facilities to underwrite publication of discographies. And the federal government, which subsidizes almost everything under the sun, can well afford to subsidize dissemination of the physical evidence, recordings, of this nation's unique art form. I find it embarrassing that foreign countries accord our jazz and popular music more significance than we do.

In today's environment minorities certainly are given aid by public and private institutions. Discographers and collectors are unquestionably a minority. Our trouble is that we are not a vocal minority. I suggest that we become vocal, that we use forums such as this Institute of Jazz Studies to advertise our needs and help satisfy our demands.

More immediately, and more realistically, there may be another approach to publication. It means going back to the commercial publisher and working more cooperatively with him. I'm now involved in this and let me tell you what's happening.

The major cost to the publisher of producing a short-run book is typesetting. If this can be eliminated, his costs fall back to that area in which he can work and at least not lose money. I've just signed a contract with a publisher to do a bio-discography on Benny Goodman.[7] I am preparing typescript that can be photographed directly. To do this I am using an IBM Selectric® typewriter that provides different type faces, and special stock designed to be used in reproduction. The manuscript I will submit will thus eliminate typesetting, make publication of this short-run book feasible for the publisher, and enable this book to be marketed in a professional manner.

Let me say, parenthetically, that this Goodman book will have as co-author Warren Hicks. When I've said "I" and "my" in relation to the book, that's my use of the egotistical first person, a new grammatical form I just invented.

The discographer cannot expect monetary reward, but I feel he should have some expectation of recovering part of his expenses. I'm not talking about a value being placed on his time; even if that were valued at only one penny per hour, his "expenses" would be considerable. I am talking about his out-of-pocket expenditures. It costs money for the author to gather his data — money for travel, money for correspondence, money for loss of vocational pay. It costs money to obtain photographs. It costs money to buy or lease special equipment, such as a special typewriter, a stereo rig, or a transcription turntable. It costs money for ribbons and special paper and a host of stenographic supplies. And, above all, it costs lots of money to accumulate the recordings.

The standard publisher's contract offers some chance of recouping a portion of these expenses. As I recall, it gives the author 10 percent of the retail selling price of the first 7,500 copies, with the percentage tilted upward slightly as the number of copies sold goes beyond 7,500. How much the author realizes is thus dependent on unit selling price and the number of copies sold; two factors which are sometimes in conflict. In the cases of the discographies I know something about, this standard contract will not enable the discographer to indulge his other hobby, a new Ferrari or even a Shelby GT500. It may permit him to get a new set of Tiger Paws for his 1964 GTO.

When and if public or private funds subsidize discographies, I hope their authors are recompensed on an entirely different basis. I think a system of direct grants might be the answer. These would allow discographers to offset their running expenses as their work progresses. At minimum, initial grants might relieve a discographer from having to make a choice between food on the table and a rare Pathe on the turntable.

Discographers, so far as I am aware, do not enter this field to make money. My start grew out of a hobby. I enjoyed the music, got some little recognition and reputation for knowing something about it, and then decided to put what I knew into print. Truthfully, money never entered my mind — until the bills started piling up. I have been conscious of it ever since, but I have not learned my lesson, and would go through the trauma of publishing a discography again, if I had to. Thanks to Warren Hicks, Arlington Press, and an IBM Selectric, I don't have to.

But I would, for there are rewards other than money. In a world whose population is now numbered in the billions, it is satisfying to possess as much as or more knowledge about a particular subject than any person in that world. It is deeply pleasing to know that something you have written is used as a reference work by collectors here and abroad, and that your book is in the libraries in Moscow, USSR, as well as Moscow, Pa. It is a renewing source of pleasure to be accepted by the artists you've written about, to be welcome in their homes, to be invited to their engagements, their celebrations, their recording sessions. It is enjoyable to make new friends because of your work. And it is gratifying to be invited to, and to belong, in an assemblage such as this today. Money or not, a regimen of cigarettes and coffee notwithstanding, it is worth it.

A final word; if you think some of the things I have said earlier are controversial, perhaps you'll consider this one even more so. And I would invite you now to participate in an open discussion about it.

Discographies published to date are merely almost computer printouts in format. Data are listed, and little more. Even the bio-discographies avoid evaluation and critical comment. I have half a mind to veer away from this in the new BG book. I am considering making judgements about musicians and their performances. I am considering including — I guess you could call them — "incidents" in part revelatory of the personalities of the artists I write about, and particularly about Benny. Not gossip, you understand, but events and his reactions to them, things like that, would be included.

And I wonder if this kind of thing falls within the purview of the discographer. Should our calling restrict us to comprehensive fact? Would we in any way jeopardize our guise as impartial observers if we venture into these other areas of subjective comment? Could, possibly, such an exercise compromise our relationships with the musicians so as to make more difficult our jobs in the future?

As I say, I am not decided on what to do. I would appreciate your comments on this subject.

REFERENCES

[1] Charles Delaunay: *Hot Discography;* Paris, 1936, 1938; New York, 1940.

[2] Brian Rust: *Jazz Records, A-Z: 1897-1931,* and *1932-1942;* Hatch End, 1962 and 1966.

[3] Luigi Sanfilippo: *General Catalog of Duke Ellington's Recorded Music:* Palermo, Italy, 1966.

[4] Stephen Wante and Walter DeBlock: *V-Disc Catalogue,* Volume 1 (Nos. 1 to 500); Antwerp, c. 1955.

[5] Howard J. Waters, Jr.: *Jack Teagarden's Music;* Stanhope, N.J., 1960.

[6] D. Russell Connor: *BG Off the Record;* Fairless Hills, Pa., 1958.

[7] D. Russell Connor and Warren W. Hicks: *BG On the Record;* New Rochelle, N.Y., 1969.

PROBLEMS OF DATING RECORDED PERFORMANCES

Carl Kendoziora
Staff Columnist, Record Research
Author and Collector

Dating recorded performances is useful as an aid in determining personnel and for chronological listing in discographies. If you know when the record was cut and what musicians were in the organization at that time, you have some information on who the soloists are.

What, then, are the methods of dating? The primary source is the record company itself. It would probably make our job almost unnecessary if all the old files existed. They do exist in more or less complete fashion in major companies like Columbia and Victor, but they don't exist at all for most of the labels that have gone out of business.

We are obliged to a number of people for what information we do have from record files. Helene F. Chmura, who used to be with Columbia, was the first person I can recall who sent out numerous detailed numerical listings of all of the masters and issues from Columbia Records. E. C. Forman of Victor was always a great help when you needed some particular information on Victor files. Decca is reluctant to cooperate with researchers; and it is unfortunate, since they have acquired so much material from old Brunswick and Vocalion catalogs. Jim Kidd in Montreal went into the files of Compo, a company which was run by the late H. S. Berliner. He found that they still had ledgers of masters from number one on up, in 92 books in the basement of the plant. This was prime source material: dates, titles, artists, etc. for the entire Compo series of recordings from 1921 to date. Jim has been making a lot of that information available.

Compo has retained a fair representation of mothers and stampers, mostly French-language material; very little jazz or American popular music. After several floods, many masters were thrown out. Someone always had the idea that the French-language material was valuable because it was unique. The rest was just "popular music," and it was not kept.

The main jazz label of Compo was Ajax, specially created by Berliner for the Negro market in the United States. He set up a small office in Chicago and most of the masters were recorded in New York. They kept the master file in New York, but when they closed the New York studio, in about 1927, the master ledgers were sent to Montreal. The office had several housecleanings and these Ajax ledgers, detailing the records by blues singers, Negro bands, and instrumentalists, were thrown out.

The Gennett Record files are another important instance. When Bill Grauer, who published the *Record Changer* magazine in the old days, made a deal with the Starr Piano Company to reissue on LPs whatever Gennett materials he could get, he went out to Richmond, Indiana, and talked to the Gennett family. They found in one of their buildings a small ledger which was Volume two of the Gennett ledgers. It started at about mid-1922 and went up to 1932, when the company ceased to record. Volume one was apparently lost, but Volume two has been the source of most of the definitive material from Gennett that is in the discographies.

Those files show that they had studios in New York and also at Richmond. The sides that were cut in New York included about 85 percent of the jazz, the main exceptions being the famous Oliver, N.O.R.K., and Morton dates. Apparently, they did not keep a separate recording ledger in New York, or they threw it out, because the bookkeepers in Richmond, who received the actual masters shipped from New York, would enter the date in the ledger in a column headed "from New York." This date was *not* the recording date, but the date on which they received the material from New York. For the sides that were cut in Richmond, the date given in the book is the recording date.

Fortunately we have been able to compare some of those "from New York" dates with authentic dates from other sources, and these "from New York" dates are from two to ten days later than the actual recording date. At least you can estimate dates within a week from this information.

After the company files and the Gennett ledgers, the next most important source of authentic accurate recording information consists of personal diaries and appointment books. Musicians, bookers, and agents have notoriously inaccurate memories. It is rare for a musician to remember accurately dates from so long ago, and even more so for bookers and agents, because they handle so many. Fortunately, there were some people who kept a written record of engagements and recording dates.

We must thank Woody Backensto of Woodbury, New Jersey, for opening up this field, because Woody, in his Red Nichols research, obtained diary information from at least two musicians: Victor D'Ippolito, a trumpeter who played with Sam Lanin and many other bands and with Red Nichols groups in the '20s and Bill Wirges, who was a band leader in the '20s.

The greatest bonanza of all was when Woody located Ed Kirkeby, famous as the manager of Fats Waller, and the manager of the California Ramblers in the '20s. He also was involved as a general booking agent for other groups and for a lot of recording engagements. He kept appointment books, which he still has, in which he listed the company they recorded for; the date and the tunes; and also, in the case of the Ramblers, the exact personnel, because he had a payroll book showing whom he paid for the engagement or recording.

A distinction must be made between a diary and an appointment book. A diary describes what *did* happen, an appointment book only what was *scheduled* to happen — regardless of whether or not the appointment was kept. In the case of a musician's diary, any title or date information that we have been able to check has been completely accurate.

In the case of appointment books such as Kirkeby's, however, there are frequent differences between what was planned and what was actually recorded. Kirkeby would contract with a company to record on, say June 10, and they might agree at that time on four particular tunes, which he would write down when he got to the studio. Kirkeby may have found that the company had recorded one tune the day before with someone else and that they wanted to do something else. Or, when they rehearsed one tune a few times, they found that it did not come off as they planned, so they substituted something else. Accordingly, we will not necessarily locate a recording of every tune that Kirkeby listed in his appointment book. We might find some sessions with different titles substituted, or sometimes with more titles or fewer titles. We usually find one or two titles that were in his book on the proper labels in the proper master series. Kirkeby's information has been quite accurate. If they were not familiar with the studio, he would give the name of the studio and the address. These books have been invaluable in dating sessions, especially for small companies for which we have no other concrete information.

There are many companies whose files are nonexistent: Pathe — Perfect, Cameo, Emerson, Plaza group, and all the little-company labels that you don't see much of any more, but were quite common in the '20s. In most cases, we had absolutely no dates for anything recorded by these companies. Now we have exact dates from Kirkeby for California Ramblers dates or Original Memphis Five dates for sessions made by these small firms. After checking out Kirkeby's information, finding titles to fit his appointment books, and assigning a date to those master numbers, we can then assign approximate dates for recordings in between, strictly by mathematical interpolation. By taking the number of masters between two known dates and dividing by the number of days, you can closely approximate the date when anything in between was recorded, usually to within a month of the actual date.

If you do not find appointment books, diaries, company files, or any other contemporary written material, you are down to release dates. There are a number of sources for release dates. *The Talking Machine World*, a trade publication on file in the New York Public Library, had a monthly section called "Advanced Record Bulletins," which listed the new releases for the coming month. For example, the June 15 issue would list the new records for July before they appeared in the stores the following month. Unfortunately, there was apparently some kind of an advertising tie-in involved. The magazine did not simply ask each company to provide its information for publication; but must have charged a fee, so many labels didn't bother with it. We are restricted, therefore, only to the labels that provided listings. Fortunately a lot of small labels did. The Plaza labels (Banner, Regal, and Domino) listed all of their releases, but Cameo only for two or three months. Over short periods Pathe listed theirs most of the time; also Gennett, Emerson, and other small labels.

Other sources of release dates are monthly throwaways and dealers' lists. The dealers' list was simply a list of the records to be issued shortly by the company and was sent to their dealers. The monthly throwaway could be picked up on the counter of a record store. They were put out each month and would list the new releases and, quite often, an alphabetical list of older ones. Dan Mahony found a complete set of Pathe-Perfect dealers' lists that someone had kept on file. That is how we were able in that Perfect catalog to complete all the listings of catalog numbers, at least the title and artist.

It is obvious that many records were recorded long before release. A Pathe dealers' list dated August might list a certain record as available to the dealer on July 15 and another record on July 1. These August releases say "available at the factory at Brooklyn" and give a still earlier date. So there you have at least six to eight weeks during which they were already in existence as a finished product, and one might ask how much before that date they actually were recorded, since the company had prepared a label copy and done all the other steps. The release dates provide at best a very rough estimate in determining the recording date. The only thing they are really good for are ceilings — an item could not have been recorded any later than the month in which it is listed as a new release.

Now we come to tune date, another very interesting facet. There is a government catalog of copyright entries in which you can find when a tune was copyrighted. One pitfall is that there may be numerous copyrights of the same tune. Sometimes each individual arrangement is copyrighted separately. However, with the earliest copyright it is fairly safe to assume that this is a floor date, and the tune was probably not recorded before its copyright (although there are exceptions). This is especially true with popular tunes. However, there might be a greater difference in dates with jazz tunes.

They might be put together on the spur of the moment, whipped into shape, recorded, and forgotten. You might never find a copyright. But if they were copyrighted, they could, and probably would, be recorded before the copyright date; the copyright being an afterthought to protect their interests.

In the record industry of the 1920s, even the smallest shoestring company still struggled to get the latest popular tunes recorded and on the market right away. If we find a date for a little company like Cardinal it is seldom more than a week behind Victor and Columbia in getting out a pop tune. They might issue fewer of the pop tunes, but they released them just as fast. To compete they had to get them out so people would buy them while the tune was at the height of its popularity.

Similar to tune dating, there are also "show" credits. A record label will frequently show it is from a certain movie or a musical comedy. This is another lead because various publications give dates when movies were released and when shows were on. Again, the company would rush to get the recording out while the show was in performance or when the movie was first released. In the '30s and '40s many times an orchestra would cut tunes from a Broadway show or movie, but they would be held back until the movie or show finally came to Broadway. I do not think that this happened in the '20s.

Another prime source is the contemporary publication. Trade magazines and newspaper files sometimes contain stories about the musicians — where they were, where they were from. If a record comes out with a suspected King Oliver solo, and you find in the paper that from October to December, 1924, King Oliver was playing in Chicago, it is unlikely that a recording made in New York during that time will have a King Oliver solo, especially in the '20s when the travel wasn't as easy as it is now.

When you are trying to date a record that you know somebody is on because it is his band or because it contains a solo obviously by this musician, and you know where that musician was at the time of recording, you may have a good clue as to when and where the record was made. Many of the smaller companies only recorded in New York, so if a band was out of New York for any period it is unlikely that they could have recorded for certain companies during that period. A few companies like Paramount and Gennett had studios in other cities beside New York, but Pathe-Perfect, Plaza (Banner, Regal, Domino), Cameo, etc., only recorded in New York. Paramount and Gennett, instead of sending out field expeditions, also had talent scouts who brought the artists into the big city studios, so that the recording locations are the same as for regular recordings.

To digress for a moment, we really have four categories of record companies in the 1920s: The majors, such as Columbia, Victor, Edison, Brunswick, Vocalion, etc.; the semi-majors, like Paramount, Gennett, and a few other companies; and two categories of the smallest–little labels which only existed over a period of less than a year or so and those which persevered the whole decade. Having a musician record only in New York would certainly apply to the smaller companies, partially to the semi-majors, and, of course, not at all to the majors. The majors had studios in many cities, and also had field trips when they took their recording equipment to where the artists were.

The final means of dating records would be contemporary accounts of recording sessions occasionally found in trade publications. A story might say that Joe Blow and his orchestra had just recorded four titles for Columbia and even, sometimes, mention the titles. This provides a date after the recording, which will vary depending on the frequency of issue of publication. If it is a magazine, the date might be four or five weeks earlier than the issue date; if it is a weekly or a daily paper, it might be a lot closer to the date of publication.

Now, let us come to the subject of recording company procedures in allocating master (or matrix) numbers. The master number is the number assigned to a specific recording by the company for purposes of identification. These were seldom chronological. If a band cut four titles with four consecutive numbers, and the next band used the next four numbers, it would be beautiful. It does not always happen that way.

The block system, for example, was used extensively by Victor and Brunswick, among others. A block of master numbers was pre-assigned to each stu-

TABLE I

A Page from the Plaza Master Files

Matrix Number	Recording Date (1925)	Title	Artist
6273	Nov. 5	*Tomorrow Mornin'*	Sam Lanin & His Orch.
6274	Nov. 5	*Don't Wait Too Long*	Sam Lanin & His Orch.
6275	Nov. 6	*You'd Never Know the Old Bunch Now*	Arthur Fields
6276	Nov. 6	*Roaming Romeo*	Arthur Fields
6277	Nov. 6	*Down Moonlight Lane*	Arthur Fields
6278	Nov. 7	*For a Girl Like You*	House band
6279	Nov. 7	*Trail of Dreams*	House band
6280	Nov. 7	*Lookin' for the One*	House band
6281	Nov. 9 (remade Dec. 8)	*I Always Think of You*	Franklyn Baur
6282	Nov. 9	*Little Love Notes*	Franklyn Baur
6283	Nov. 9	*Bonita*	Franklyn Baur
6284	Nov. 10	*Steppin' Fool*	Perry's Hot Dogs
6285	Nov. 10	*I'm Gonna Hang Around My Sugar*	Perry's Hot Dogs
6286	Nov. 10	*Charlestonette*	Perry's Hot Dogs
6287	Nov. 10	*Cu-Kee-Ukee-Ute*	Boyd Senter
6288	Nov. 10	*Ole Crow Blues*	Boyd Senter
6289			
6290	Nov. 17	*No Man's Mama*	Lou Gold & His Orch.
6291	Nov. 13	*Someone's Stolen My Sweet Sweet Baby*	Ben Selvin & His Orch.
6292	Nov. 17	*Roll 'em Girls*	Lou Gold and His Orch.
6293	Nov. 26 (16?)	*Sleepy Time Gal*	Fletcher Henderson & H. Orch.
6294	Nov. 12	*Whoopee!*	Eddie Peabody & His Band
6295	Nov. 12	*Clap Hands! (Here Comes Charley!)*	Eddie Peabody & His Band
6296	Nov. 13	*A Little Bungalow*	Ben Selvin & His Orch.
6297	Nov. 16	*Then I'll Be Happy*	Fletcher Henderson & Orch.
6298 (remade Dec. 5)	Nov. 17	*Song of the Vagabonds*	Lou Gold & His Orch.

dio that recorded for them. Victor was notorious in that respect. Unless you know where they were cut you can't estimate dates from the numbers. For instance, master 40500 was the beginning of a block assigned to the New York studio. They sent the 40700's to Camden and 40800's and 40900's to Chicago. When New York ran out of numbers, they skipped over the ones assigned to Camden and Chicago and started a new block at 41000 so that the master numbers are chronological only within the same studio. This is impossible to tell without other company information. (Rust's new *Victor Master Book* is invaluable source material.) Even the company that recorded in one studio did not always assign masters in strict chronological order.

Table I is a page from the Plaza master files of records that came out on the Banner, Regal, Domino, Oriole, Jewel, Challenge, and other labels. From 6273 to 6288 the list is in chronological order.

Please note 6281, a remake. Master 6281 was originally recorded on November 9, 1925, and remade on December 8. We do not know how many times they cut it each time. If we find a record of that particular tune with that master number and it is take-2 or take-3, we cannot be sure which session it is from. They might have cut anywhere from two to five takes during each session. The take number at which you can fix it at the earlier date, rather than the remake date, is purely conjecture.

To continue with the list, we get out of chronological order. At 6289 there is one blank number which was not assigned, not used, or not entered. Then there are various masters by Lou Gold, Ben Selvin, Fletcher Henderson, and Eddie Peabody. There seems to be no reason for this. Why is one master cut four days earlier than the one before it? One theory is that the company may have allotted master numbers to the band before they arrived. They may have booked in advance, as shown by Kirkeby's appointment books. They may have made an arrangement with the booker to cut four titles so they assigned four masters to use in recording that band when it arrived, and then the next four masters to another band. When the first band came in, they may have cut only three masters and run out of time, or somebody got sick. Now they had a blank master which may have been assigned to somebody else, out of chronological order, or which may have been skipped. Conversely, they may have cut more titles than they planned, and, having allotted masters for the next band coming in, they may have had to skip ahead several numbers to get an unused master number for the extra title.

As far as the record company is concerned, the only use that the master numbers have is to distinguish one recording from another. They are not concerned with chronological order. Those of us who are trying to untangle it are frustrated by these idiosyncracies. We don't know why this happens, but it does happen, and that is why we have to be cautious in assigning dates to masters, even when we know the dates for masters in the vicinity.

I would like to show you one more interesting fact involving remakes, which can confuse discographers. You may find a perfectly normal-looking record attributed to a certain orchestra, but it is a great disappointment because it doesn't sound like that orchestra. A typical case is that of masters 6311 and 6312, dated November 27, 1925, "Who" and "Spanish Shawl" by Fletcher Henderson and his Orchestra, both have numbers which say, "remade, December 14." The remakes were by some different group, not Henderson, and these were the takes that were issued, even though Henderson's name was retained on the label for some issues.

It is unfortunate that some companies made a habit of remaking a master and using the same master number, even though they changed the artist. In some cases, the office help were apparently not informed and would use the credit as given for the original master number. If anywhere in the world there is a pressing of take-1 of either of those titles, it's probably Fletcher Henderson. But takes-4, -5, and -6 were issued, and these are obviously not Henderson.

Companies had different systems for handling remakes. Some of them, including Pathe, would assign a new master number to a remake. Most companies simply gave it a higher take number using the old master number, as in the Henderson examples. Many times they would change the artists, which creates a lot of confusion. As a specific example, there is a Columbia record by Clara Smith, with "Kansas City Man Blues" on one side. The label reads: Stanley Miller, piano accompaniment on one side, and Fletcher Henderson on the other side. Actually, it's Fletcher on both sides. The reason for error is that Stanley Miller made the original takes of that one side which were never issued. Henderson did the remake, as well as the other side, which was cut at the same time as the remake; so Henderson is on both sides. It is a fifth take of the remade title. But the Columbia files and record labels apparently didn't note that change of piano players.

I might also mention the Paramount 800 block. This is a unique situation because Paramount's masters are usually chronological, except for this group of numbers beginning at about 800. We suspected that they were not chronological because 800 series numbers appeared in the catalog series after many of the 900 and 1000 series numbers were already appearing. It was not until the Kirkeby appointment books were unearthed that we found proof. These are dates for artists he booked for Paramount: Charles Harrison, the California Ramblers, Arthur Fields, Monroe Silver, the comedian, etc. Table II lists the masters for those titles as taken from the records after we found them. Note that 842 was recorded between 985 and 994. For some unknown reason the Paramount 800's were being cut over a different time period than the rest of the master series.

Paramount was a culprit in another respect. In the later '20s they adopted master series at random, tired of them very quickly, and went on to different ones. They would start a certain thousand block and never get up to 099 before starting a different thousand. There are masters of the 4000s, 5000s, 6000s, 9000s, 10000s and all others, few of which ever get above the first hundred. One specific example that proves how they operated was Paramount 12250 by Thelma Vizzo. There were two titles cut at the same recording session, since it is obviously the same group on both sides. One matrix is 9099 and the other is 10000. For unknown reasons, when they reached 9099, instead of going to 9100 they started at 10000 with a new block.

TABLE II
PARAMOUNT MATRIX LISTING

Matrix No.	Rec. Date	Title	Artist
764	6/27/21	*Cohen at the Telephone*	Monroe Silver
765	6/27/21	*Cohen the Politician*	Monroe Silver
766	6/28/21	*A Little Love*	Adler Trio
767	6/28/21	*Herd Girl's Dream*	Adler Trio
800	(released Sept. 1920)	*Blues*	White Way Jazz Band
801	(released Sept. 1920)	*Tiger Rag*	White Way Jazz Band
842	2/9/22	*Molly-O*	Arthur Fields
900	(released c. Nov. 1921)	*Baltimore*	Hobart Smock
914	10/17/21	*Love Will Find a Way*	Charles Harrison
938	11/23/21	*That's How I Believe In You*	Charles Harrison
939	11/23/21	*I Want My Mammy*	Arthur Fields
974	1/20/22	*Kathleen Mavourneen*	Hugh Donovan
975	1/20/22	*Come Back to Erin*	Hugh Donovan
979	1/30/22	*Granny*	California Ramblers
980	1/30/22	*My Mammy Knows*	California Ramblers
985	1/30/22	*While Miami Dreams*	California Ramblers
994	2/20/22	*Cohen at the Wedding*	Monroe Silver

The prime take number systems are simple: -1, -2, -3, or A, B, and C after a master number. Thus the given number with A or -1 is the first take, B or -2 is the second, and so on. Gennett had a unique system. They used the ABC designation but their first take had *no letter*, so that A is actually the second take and take B is the third and so on. In the Gennett ledgers they refer to that take without a letter as "plain." Why they had to do that to confuse the discographer I don't know, but, luckily, the ledgers prove that that was their system. Each letter was, therefore, one take later than it would indicate from its numerical position in the alphabet.

Then we have companies like Brunswick and Vocalion, which used a separate master for every take. You have no way of knowing which take you have unless you know how many numbers were assigned to that title, and you have to have recording company information before you could know which take you had. Fortunately, a lot of that material is available, the range of masters assigned to a given title being listed in most discographies. However, Brunswick threw a stumbling block into that by not putting the masters on most of their pressings, or, at best, using only the last two digits of the master number.

There was a unique system used by a small company in Albany, the Federal Record Company. It used a combination of these two systems. They used a separate master for each take, but they also showed which take it was as a prefix numeral. In that way you could fill in a lot of missing master numbers without seeing the records. If you found a record with, say, 3-1800 on it, you knew that 1800 was the third take of that title. Therefore, 1799 and 1798 were takes two and one, respectively. The higher the take number, the more numbers you could assign to that title, and you did not have to find every master and every take pressed on the records before you could enter it into your book.

Then we have a problem which, I believe, Howard Waters was the first to unravel. The Pathe company had a unique system of recording their original masters onto a cylinder; not a small familiar Edison cylinder, but a large cylinder, about a foot long and five or six inches in diameter. They then transferred them, mechanically, to a lateral master, and then to all size records. They had a special 16-inch high RPM record which they produced for ballrooms, and they had a special phonograph to play it. By spreading the grooves of an ordinary three-minute recording far enough apart to fill a 16-inch disc, they could get tremendous modulation. This was a mechanical dubbing process — no more, no less. If you have hi-fi equipment and play a Pathe or Perfect record, as soon as you put your needle down you hear a dubbing hiss above the hiss of the actual playing of the record.

They had a system of numbering their takes which was most complicated. If they transferred only one take of a recording made at a particular session, they gave it a master number, a dash, and a number. That number after the dash was not a take number, but a transfer number. They sometimes transferred from the cylinder three or four different times. I don't know what they were trying to achieve in those mechanical days, but we know that one of the faults of some transfers was simply that they didn't leave enough blank grooves before the music started. There is a certain record that was either -1, -2, -4, -5, or some other number, but never -3. A test with -3 has a scribbled note on the blank label, "It starts too soon." When it is played the music starts before it gets a whole turn around. So they never used that transfer because it was defective.

But all of those dash numbers were identical performances, not different takes. When they transferred more than one take of a master to lateral discs, they had to show which was which. If you find a little letter over the dash, like a master number with an A over the dash, another one with B over the dash, those were alternates; not necessarily takes one and two because they apparently just numbered the transfers A and B. They might actually have been takes -3 and -4. After Pathe went electrical in later years, they adopted the normal system of the dash number as a true take.

I will finish with a little music which might show you a classic example of what can happen with a remake by a different band. The Ben Pollack band, with Benny Goodman, recorded two titles that are involved here on two different dates. The original version was cut by Pollack on February 12, 1931. It was remade on March 2, again by Pollack, and then it was remade a second time, on March 18 by Ed Kirkeby's California Ramblers. We are not sure which takes are from which dates because we do not know how many takes were cut at each date. But, it is quite obvious that take -10 is Kirkeby's, made on the third date. All the copies of that record that you will find are labeled Ben Pollack and his Orchestra, vocal chorus by Ben Pollack. No one has ever seen one labeled Ed Kirkeby. Yet, almost all copies of the record are take -10, the Kirkeby version. But there are one or two copies of the Pollack versions in collections; one copy, on Perfect, is take-5 on both sides. Another copy is take-4 on one title and take-6 on the other: they are obviously Pollack because it is Pollack singing, Teagarden on trombone, Goodman on clarinet. I will conclude by playing one of the titles, "Sweet and Hot." On the tape I have takes-4 and -5 by the Pollack band, as labeled, and take-10, the Kirkeby remake. You will hear the difference, but all the record label credits are identical, as I have described.

REFERENCES

Carl Kendoziora and Perry Armagnac: *Perfect Dance and Race Catalogue (1922-1930);* Record Research, Nos. 51/52, May/June 1963.

Brian Rust: *The Victor Master Book,* Vol. 2; Hatch End, 1969.

PROBLEMS OF IDENTIFYING PERFORMERS

Howard Waters
Author, Jack Teagarden's Music

I would like to review, briefly, the beginnings of discography and mention that the earliest research in personnel and soloist identification was limited in its purpose. It was done, primarily, I think, by the jazz fan, the listening collector — as opposed to the collector who merely accumulates records. He was interested in finding out whom he was hearing. In the early '30s serious research was unknown, and there was little concern for the detail and accuracy which we have come to expect and demand.

As the influence of jazz spread around the world and jazz was commercially exploited, the demand for knowledge increased as its audience expanded. The demand, which centered around knowing who the performers were and something about them, attracted writers — some who were qualified to write about jazz and others who were not. Publications devoted to jazz and discography elevated jazz to the concert hall and often gave jazz musicians employment. Record collectors appeared in increasing numbers in the later '30s, and collecting became a hobby as listening to jazz had become the hobby of the earlier collectors.

Therefore, when we discuss why are we interested in identifying performers, we are really talking about levels of listening. All of us are acquainted with different collectors, fans, and people interested in jazz. They don't listen in the same way, but vary from the concerned listener who is uninterested in original labels, original pressings, and accumulating a large stock of records, to the research-oriented person who is absorbed in research as an end in itself. The documentation of facts, almost without regard to their relationship to the music, is so absorbing to some people that they miss the value in music. Fortunately, there are collectors who do listen, and I think that they have brought about many of the changes in research.

In the last 20 years we have witnessed an increasing awareness, among commercial record companies, of the demands of the collector. I think that the companies have catered to these demands, in some cases, because they could develop a market of collectors who identified with artists, and it was good business to include personnel data on record sleeves. In other cases there are informed and sophisticated individuals within the companies who are interested in music themselves and have exerted influence on their companies.

If we ask ourselves why we are interested in the identification of personnel, we have to be a little introspective. Why is it important to us, as individuals, to know who is playing? What benefit do we gain from research that may tell us the names of people long dead who made records 20, 30, or 40 years ago? Does it in some way enhance our enjoyment of the music? Even if the answer to that question is no, I suspect we probably prefer to think that it does enhance our appreciation.

I think it is partly instinctive for us to want to identify with a performer that we admire or respect. By knowing the names of performers whose music we enjoy, we feel something of a kinship, perhaps a harmless form of hero worship.

In addition, there is simple curiosity which brings out the scientific streak in some of us. This inquisitiveness urges us to acquire knowledge as well as records, and it affects us, especially, when we possess or know something that we think others do not. It gives us a certain status within ourselves.

But there are better reasons for seeking knowledge which can be justified in terms of the music alone. Jazz is, by its nature, a personal expression of individuals in musical form, and it demands freedom of expression. When jazz musicians are free to express themselves, it is as if they were speaking spontaneously to the listener who can hear and appreciate. And the instrumental jazz voice is, I think, as unique and direct a form of communication as the spoken word. Through music, it is able to convey thoughts and feelings, which might be difficult or impossible to express verbally.

If we accept that, we might ask, "Who among us, when spoken to, does not want to know who is speaking?" Where the personal communication is most direct in music, such as in small groups where the individual musician has the most opportunity to be inventive, creative, and expressive, the listener can distinguish and appreciate the individual contributions of each musician; and identifying them has greater meaning. In larger groups, such as big bands, musicians tend to lose their identity and the value of their identification is less. Their technical competence and interpretive capability may be interesting when comparing two symphony orchestras, but beyond mere technical ability, much depends upon the conductor. When we consider the soloist, who has maximum individual freedom, and whose communication is most direct, we become more concerned with knowing the performer's identity.

There are many among us who wonder what qualifies experts in discography to identify musicians. What establishes their credibility? There are no absolute rules of criteria, but certain attributes, such as the scientific attitude, and a questioning frame of mind, are necessary; the ability continually to review and evaluate findings; to discriminate between fact and judgement; to resist making errors of assumption; to accept new evidence, and to evaluate it impartially.

A formal background in music is an advantage, I believe, but I seriously doubt that it qualifies one to identify personnel. The development and training of the ear requires a basic sensitivity to pitch, vibrato, and rhythm, but it also requires a reliable musical memory. All aural identification must be made by comparing sounds with other known sounds previously stored in a musical memory that is developed over a long period of listening. With the capacity for storing and cataloging musical images, a musical memory functions in the same way as a computer. It stores, it recalls, it compares, and it makes determinations.

Today, in the field of personnel identification, as in other areas of discography, there is a trend toward specialization by identifying one artist or a group of related artists. This specialization has a certain disadvantage because experts may work in all areas of personnel identification, but do not necessarily exchange information. Nevertheless, specialization is necessary because the depth of knowledge and experience required in making personnel identifications is such that one person is not likely to be competent to make identifications in all areas of jazz. Also, we are all limited by time and must concentrate our efforts.

Publishing a list of all the records by a particular artist and calling it a complete discography is no longer sufficient. The field of bio-discography is just opening up and we should concentrate our effort on expanding its coverage.

There are several sources of personnel information. Recording company files are an invaluable source, if the recording company maintained them. However, you probably will not find personnel listings prior to 1940. Only recently have record companies published personnel data for their customers, and it was done because they found it commercially profitable.

Record labels as a source of personnel data did not become of any value until the mid-'30s, and even they can be in error. Payroll records are an excellent source—Ed Kirkeby's personnel files and payroll books, which amount to a personnel listing of his recordings, is a good example. The date books of musicians, leaders, and bookers occasionally include personnel records. However, these three types of sources are extremely rare and must be supplemented by other sources such as interviews, news accounts, trade publications, popular magazines, periodicals, films, and photographs. These latter sources, films and photographs, have only begun to be explored. Data from musicians, either by personal interview or by mail questionnaire, is valuable, but should be elicited by sound interview techniques to be reliable. The interview has other pitfalls such as memory loss by subject, the lapse of time since the event, the amount of recording activity by the musician, and the constant changes in his music associations. These occupational characteristics tend to confuse the memory. When I compiled the book on Jack Teagarden it was a revelation to look at the partial itinerary I was able to put together. It was obvious that after years of one-nighters, asking any musician to recall the presence or absence of a specific individual on a particular day at a particular time would be almost a joke.

Having a musician listen to recordings and identify performers is very risky. A musician's musical memory of how his associates sounded on record 30 years ago is hardly reliable. This opinion is worth having and evaluating, but the real problem comes when the interviewer accepts the opinion as fact.

I would like to mention a little-known technique which was suggested to me some years ago, and, as far as I know, is still untested. I understand that in an hypnotic trance one could be transported back to a particular time and place. If some of the old-timers were hypnotized and returned to the recording studio, perhaps they could give us information that might be worth documenting.

Also, there have been reports of a new machine which identifies persons by their voices. It may be used by the telephone companies to trace crank calls and to identify people in the same way that fingerprints are used. The idea of using such a device to identify personnel and soloist is intriguing and worthy of investigation.

The hardest, most controversial, part of personnel identification is using the aural method. Identification is based upon a mental comparison of an unidentified sound with the stored memory of various sounds and making a judgement as to whether the two are or are not identical. This is the basic technique. The fact that we may know the name of the musicians who produced the sound stored in our memory is not essential to the process of comparison. On what basis do we make this comparison? What characterizes the sound and enables us to distinguish one from another? There are various qualities: tone, vibrato, timbre, pitch, intonation, attack, articulation, phrasing, the voicing of chords, particularly in the arranging and piano; and the content of the playing. There are melodic, harmonic, and rhythmic patterns and personal devices which are part of a musician's personal style such as trills, shakes, and smears. Perhaps the most important of all, and the hardest to describe, is the feel — the subtle emotional quality which is personal to each musician and, perhaps, unique to jazz expression.

I would like to mention some of the factors which can favorably influence making an accurate identification and others which may be handicaps. A factor which should have a helpful influence is our prior knowledge of the circumstances surrounding a particular recording date; the known presence or absence of certain musicians in the city or recording location; the professional or personal associations of specific musicians other than on recording dates; where, when, and with whom these musicians were working on their regular jobs. It is not uncommon for musicians to double on more than one job at a time in hotels, clubs, radio, and TV. Knowing leaders' preferences is useful. Usually every leader uses free-lance men and has his choices, first call, and so on. This could be especially important when the leader is free-lancing himself and must develop a group composed entirely of free-lance musicians.

Before attempting an aural identification it is important that we have stored in our musical memory sufficient examples of reliably identified musicians. Without a reliable basis for comparison, the effort to make any sort of valid comparison and subsequent identification is wasted. And, if the entire basis for our comparison (that which is stored in our musical memory) is in error, then we are lost. Too often the recorded examples we should be able to use for reference are too limited in number or wrongly identified in our references. The result is not only wasted time and effort, but a confusion which is compounded when erroneous conclusions are published. They, in turn, may be used as references, and the situation compounds itself. As we all know, retracting erroneous data is often serious, difficult, and in some respects impossible.

There are always researchers who will use outdated references. It is almost as if time had passed them by, and erroneous information is difficult to erase from memory.

Or, the researcher may be operating within too limited a musical universe; i.e., he may lack listening experience and be unable to hear the distinctions he seeks to hear. For example, it has been assumed for years that Red Nichols made thousands of records in the '20s, when in fact, he was not present on a large proportion of those with which he has been credited.

Without knowing it, the researcher may have an underlying desire to prove or disprove the presence or absence of certain musicians. If he is a Benny Goodman collector, he may subconsciously hope that each newly-found record contains his favorite and is easily convinced because he wants to be. There are pitfalls in other unconscious reactions. For example, assumptions that all data in print are true, or that certain musicians were always together on recordings, are dangerous. We are all familiar with the Nichols-Mole syndrome, the Goodman-Teagarden association, the Dorsey Brothers, et al. In fact, Red Nichols and Miff Mole recorded separately more than they recorded together, and, perhaps, the same could be said of the Dorsey brothers, Benny Goodman, and Jack Teagarden.

One minor point: listening to records for an aural identification requires some orientation to the general style of music of the period. Musical cliches have been used, and one must be familiar with them before recognizing individual contributions. One must recognize the recorded sound of the period, perhaps even to the differences in sound between companies. In the '20s this was more important because recording techniques varied between companies.

Finally, when comparing one musician with another we should bear in mind the changes that affect a musician's performance. Over any period of time, techniques improve. Particularly in the '20s, many of the most admired jazz musicians were very young and their techniques were in a formative stage. Differences are often apparent in records made two or three years apart. The musician's association with others or with those who influence him and his style, his own adaptation to changes in general musical trends, and his own personal maturity are factors which can almost produce two different identities for the same musician over a period of only a few years.

I think that we have reached a point today when the studious, serious researcher has so much data available that he may learn and absorb more information in less time than ever before. Progress during the last decade or so indicates that today's researchers are far better equipped to use available techniques, and have a better understanding of the problems of discographical research, particularly, in the identification of personnel.

I also believe that today's researchers are more seriously dedicated to unraveling the mysteries of personnel than ever before. They are not satisfied with automatically accepting the findings of their predecessors, and this is a healthy sign. There are far too many errors in existing references, and, by continuing to question and reevaluate evidence, the truth may someday be found and accepted. However, since much of what we do must depend on subjective judgement and aural identification, the eternal question will be: when can opinion be accepted as fact? At what point do we stop questioning subjective judgements? We must learn to live with problems which are not subject to scientific solution. Discography and the identification of personnel, soloists in particular, will always remain an inexact science. Yet by serious application of all the research techniques at our disposal, I believe we can reduce the areas of uncertainty to a meaningless few. It is a gradual process of refinement in which I think we all must play a part.

JAZZ AND SOCIAL SCIENCE

Charles Nanry
Assistant Professor of Sociology
Rutgers University

Jazz is an attractive art form. Its attraction, however, varies insofar as those who come to jazz bring a variety of talents with them. Some participants in the jazz life are artists, some are businessmen, some are collectors, and still others are scholars.

This last category has been dominated by historians, but there is a real need for others with specialized skills to apply those special skills to jazz. In modern, urban, specialized society there is a need for every group to employ specialists to deal with the complexities of the modern world. A jazz musician should *not* be expected to be a discographer, but he might very well expect a discographer to provide him with the specialized information that he needs to grow as an artist. For example, a carefully selected tape of trumpet solos from King Oliver to Don Cherry might be most useful to any student of the jazz trumpet.

But discography is not the only area where specialists might be useful. There is a great need in jazz for an economist to study seriously the economics of the jazz life. A study of economic structure of night clubs, for example, would be most useful. You all know that there is a strange mystique about how a night club operates. Night club owners are often considered terrible people—which they may be or may not be. There is the notion among some musicians that club owners are making millions of dollars from the labor of the poor musician. The musician often regards the club owner with suspicion and hostility. What is the real economic structure of a night club? How does it operate? Does anyone really know? There is a need for certain professions, including economics, to devote a few of their members, at least, to a serious study of this vital art form.

There is a general need to know better the structure of the performing arts. It does little good for musicians and promoters to condemn each other while work contexts diminish. A jazz musician cannot be expected to learn all about the discipline of economics, but an economist should be able to teach any musician enough specialized economics for his own survival.

There are other academic areas whose contribution to jazz need not be purely academic. Political scientists might help in setting up a "jazz lobby." Psychologists ought to explore the jazz experience from their perspective. I hardly need emphasize to this audience the critical importance of serious historical analysis. More musicological research is needed as well as the coordination of discographical work. Many specialized laborers are needed in the vineyard — it is the eleventh hour.

But permit me to speak about my own discipline, sociology. I have conducted research into jazz as an occupation[1]. I attempted to develop a sociological perspective on what it means to be a jazz musician. The study is of currently working musicians. Historical data are used to fill in some of the background about the jazz occupation and what that occupational life is like. I am an occupational sociologist. I had been working in this area for several years prior to my sociological interest in jazz. I wanted to apply some of the knowledge to the jazz life.

In a sense, my own research is constructed as a kind of mosaic in which I have applied bits and pieces of information that have been gathered by other researchers on other occupations like medicine, law, factory work, and even railroading, to jazz musicians. We need to know what work means to jazz people and why they work as they do. In order to understand the jazz life better I have had to find out what the jazz occupation is. This was the first problem, and almost an insurmountable one, because there really are two very different ways to approach jazz as an occupation.

One is to take an *a priori* approach, i.e., work up a definition of jazz and then consider only those people who fit that definition. I tried that for about six months and could find almost no agreement about what jazz music really is and who "true" jazz musicians are. So I had to develop a more empirical strategy.

The strategy I chose was to allow people to define themselves. People who say they are jazz musicians are considered jazz musicians. At what point would they no longer be able to support that self-definition? One of the most interesting early discoveries that I made in my research is that a jazz musician is almost totally dependent upon his fellow jazz musicians for his *social* self-definition.

Unless the jazz self-definition is maintained by the people who surround him, a jazz musician will not be able to maintain that definition and will eventually drop out; he will become a laughingstock. Everybody will know that he is not really a jazz musician. He will not be able to follow that particular vocation without support from others. Following this same lead, the next problem considered was the mechanism through which the jazz self-definition is maintained for an individual.

One of the interesting discoveries here is that, like so many other occupations, the way in which the jazz musician maintains his self-definition as a jazz man is through hiring practices.

A musician maintains his jazz self-definition by being hired by other jazz musicians who call him on a gig. That way he assures himself and others that he is really what he thinks he is. If a man does not get called over a period of months or years, he begins to lose this feeling of himself as a jazz musician. Because hiring practices within jazz are so important to this research, I developed a full-blown questionnaire and depth interview schedule in which I talked to a wide variety of musicians of various types to try and find out exactly how hiring practices work in the real world.

One important finding was that the two most important dimensions in defining what styles of music a man will play and how he maintains his jazz self-definition are age and race.

There tends to be clique formation among musicians who are in about the same age group. Jazz styles are highly correlated with age cohorts. There also tends to be closure around a style so that there are many separate traditions in jazz. Jazz is a multi-layered kind of occupation in which there are many age-specific jazz styles.

Race intrudes on the jazz life in ways that are analogous to the intrusion of age; we are all painfully aware of racism in jazz.[2] But the racial dimension also introduces subtle differences since racial cliques, like age cliques, inhibit interaction and, through partial isolation, lead to stylistic differences.

I have asked many young musicians what kinds of groups they play with, or get involved with; what kinds of jazz they play, and so on. Young musicians often play with the people who are around them. Physically it is very difficult for a group of black kids from Jamaica to go out to Long Island to play with a group of white kids. So, the white kids tend to play together, the black kids tend to play together, and this is reflected in their jazz. The norm of tolerance which, it is said, runs through jazz and the idea that there is a great deal of integration must be investigated. Jazz is more segregated than integrated. For some musicians this is due, in part at least, to patterns of residential segregation.

From an empirical point of view, I have tried to look at some of the clubs in New York and take a long-range sample to see just how much integration exists. In sampling one series of jazz concerts in a major New York jazz club over a period of three years I found that more than 80 percent of the groups that played were *not* integrated. I am applying the same criterion to age integration. The ages of the men who play together tend to be fairly close. There are major exceptions to this. There are certain key people in the jazz occupation who hire young men to introduce *a la* Chico Hamilton or Horace Silver. But most players give jobs to their friends.

I have also found, interestingly enough, that some of the better known informal aspects of jazz are dying. It was once standard operating procedure for a young musician to come into town, his horn under his arm, and try to find a bunch of guys blowing somewhere and sit in with them. If he was good, his reputation was made; if he was not, be went back to Miami (or wherever) and woodshedded for another year, came back and tried again. Or he did not come back at all. The jam session and the practice of sitting in are declining very rapidly. Formal criteria are beginning to replace informal criteria in the jazz occupation. This is a very old theme in the sociology of occupations. The idea of professionalism, i.e., having the proper credentials, the proper degrees, and having the right jazz masters as teachers, and so on, is beginning to replace the model of the player showing up with hayseed in his hair and a horn under his arm and knocking everybody dead. There are changes going on within the occupation and we again see distinct differences, depending on the particular age group and social category within jazz that we are looking at. This is one of the things that I am trying to delineate in my own researches: how this process goes on and what its identifiable patterns are.

There is also a major problem in the jazz occupation which is not unique to jazz, but is unique to certain types of occupations, particularly artistic occupations. That problem flows from the fact that the jazz musician himself has very little economic control over his own occupation. The control of the occupation is lodged outside the professional group and this is difficult for groups that purport to be fully professional and autonomous. No outsider tells doctors how to be doctors or lawyers how to be lawyers. In other words, there are very strong professional associations and organizations which define codes of ethics and practices for these established professional groups from within the profession itself. There is no such thing for the jazz musician and this constitutes one of his fundamental problems in leading the jazz life.

He depends on fellow jazz musicians for his self-image, for a kind of social self, but he also has to depend economically on outsiders who really may have very little empathy with what real jazz is. In the words of one club owner I interviewed: "I like all kinds of music but my favorite kind of music is the sound of the cash register ringing." This is the sort of man who controls the economic aspects of the musician's life. The musician is really part of a schizoid world in which he is trying to balance the social support that he needs from his fellow jazz musicians with the economic support that he needs from outsiders who may not have any sympathy or empathy with the kind of music that he is trying to produce.

There is a dynamic tension within jazz that may even account for some of its stylistic aspects. Jazz is a profession that, in some respects at least, cannot set its own rules, and this creates difficulties. It is a profession that is beginning to make stumbling attempts towards formalization and professionalization, which may or may not be good for the creative aspects of the occupation in the long run.

I have also begun to do some research on the role of the musicians' union for the jazzman. There has been a very strange kind of relationship between the jazz artists and the musicians' union. The American Federation of Musicians, in particular, Local 802 in New York, is really set up on the AFL craft model. Those who run the union often see the musicians in the same way that other craft unions see carpenters, plumbers, or any other kind of craftsmen, while the musician may see himself as an artist, not primarily as a performer. The musician's self-image may be that of a creator and all that that implies. He is being treated, however, as a craftsman by a union using the same model that could be used for plumbers. He gets so much an hour, 15 minutes on, 15 minutes off, all kinds of rules and regulations which the jazzman is not really very open to. The jazz musician has had very little to say about how the union is structured. He has never had any real power within the union, never had any control over the way in which the union operates. The control is generally lodged in the hands of professionals who have really made their lives in the world of labor unions rather than the world of music.

In interviewing some of the top echelon people at 802 for example, I found that few of them played music professionally. Most of the officers were lawyers or had been involved in the labor movement of the '30s. They got into the musicians' union not because they were musicians, but because they were in the labor movement. This was another AFL affiliate that they could go to. Again you see another aspect of the musician's life, another kind of conflict being built in.

I am beginning to suspect that many musicians do accept their imposed self-image as craftsmen. This is partly a result of the union structure, and partly a result of the dominance of the recording studio over work contexts in recent years. The self-fulfilling prophecy may be at work here, i.e., the musician is cast in the role that his union sets for him.

What I hope I have done is to give you a glimpse into the kind of work that I am doing here at Rutgers. Until recently I think it has been fairly rare for people with academic credentials to devote themselves to a life of research about jazz unless they happen to be jazz musicians or they do it on a part-time basis. Even that is an unusual circumstance.

Most other major art forms have their historians and now they have picked up psychologists and sociologists and other specialists who have become interested in the art form and devote themselves to a life of study of it. This has been very unusual in jazz. I think you people here today represent a kind of jazz underground, the people who have been doing the research, doing the kind of thing that historians and others should have been doing and hopefully will be doing in the future.

There is a great amateur tradition, especially in discographical research, of a lot of people overlapping in the kind of work they are doing. Sometimes there is lack of communication about what is being done. It is my hope, and it is the collective hope of all of us here at Rutgers, that with the Institute lodged in a major university, and with the cooperation of other like-minded institutes and collections in other universities, we can begin to focus some serious scholarly research on various aspects of jazz. Whether it is occupational studies or psychological studies of jazz, social psychological studies of jazz, or economic surveys, now is the time to induce professions in various disciplines to come to jazz and to display new facets, to shed new light on jazz from their particular points of view.

I think it is a tremendous tribute to Marshall Stearns and to his persistence that he was able to do the tremendous amount of work that he did in jazz. How much better it would have been if he could have had a full-time appointment as professor of jazz at Hunter College rather than making jazz a part-time thing. I have no idea what he would have wanted in this regard, but we should have the opportunity to have jazz chairs opened up in the same way we have serious research in other artistic forms. The hour is late, the vines are heavy with fruit.

REFERENCES

[1]See: Nanry, Charles, "The Occupational Subculture of the Jazz Musician: Myth and Reality", 1970, unpublished Ph.D. dissertation, Rutgers University. (Available from University Microfilms, Ann Arbor); Nanry, Charles, "Jazz and All That Sociology" in *American Music from Storyville to Woodstock,* Transaction Books, Charles Nanry, Editor, (forthcoming, 1971).

[2]For the best scholarly discussion of this see: Morroe Berger, "Jazz Resistance to the Diffusion of a Culture-Pattern," *The Journal of Negro History,* Vol. XXXII, No. 4, October, 1947.

June 21, 1969

SECTION II

Second Annual Conference on Discographical Research

THE BIRTH OF DISCOGRAPHY

Rudi Blesh
Author of Shining Trumpets,
They All Played Ragtime (in collaboration with Harriet Janis);
Consultant on oral history project with Eubie Blake

Some people would question my qualifications to keynote this conference of discographers — those scholars who, by serving many masters, end by serving none. Those questioners would be right; my strictly discographical qualifications are in the immediate neighborhood of zero. Though I have come to admire the qualities that active discographical research requires, I do not possess them. Precision, endless patience, tireless hewing and assembling of the minute building blocks called facts or data, laying them in ashlar rows, tearing down, then again rebuilding an endless structure called statistical accuracy — this is an activity I still view with astonishment.

But that astonishment, which twenty-five or thirty years ago was mixed with a kind of deprecatory amusement, is today composed only of admiration. For it is within that evergrowing structure called statistical truth that history has her safe living quarters.

A generation ago — when that new thing, jazz, was where it was — we dropouts used to laugh at our "in" jokes and legends which had versions to fit each one's Own Thing. Here was one: if you would listen very carefully to a scratchy, secondhand shellac disk with a Claxtonola label, bearing a certain take of a tune played by Boyd Senter and His Senterpedes, you would hear amid the needle hiss a faraway, faint "Kerchoo!" The sneeze, of course (as any hepcat knew), was a rare lick by a cornetist name of Beiderbecke. Bix just happened to be in the Claxtonola studio just visiting, or (poor Bix!) waiting until Boyd received the loot in order to put the bite on him for a fifth of bootleg Gordon's gin.

Someone, however, in our generation, by intense, concentrated listening, heard that sneeze that everyone else had either missed or dismissed. And it was a lively imagination and built-in love of lore and legend that created a new myth to add to the legend of a gifted, twenty-eight-year-old Iowa boy who had just died, the best of his music still unplayed.

That whole Boyd Senter bit is laughable, perhaps, but, in its fullest sense, not trivial. To create it required a sensitivity to implication, an awareness of possibilities in the jazz scene at that time. And that situation was nothing if not extraordinary. Here was a native, quasi-folk music that was a fine, but virtually unrecognized, creative art. At the same time it was both a product of uniquely American social forces and, itself, a strong social force. It was rich and significant material for musicologist, folk-lorist, psychologist, sociologist, esthetician, and historian. But nobody was having any. Jazz, the mother lode, went untouched. Rejected out of hand by the Establishment, it was unchronicled history vanishing day by day. As Bessie Smith sang: "Nobody knows where I comes from/Nobody knows my name."

It was a time when jazz and its wonderful protective vessel, the 78 rpm shellac disk, were truly terra incognita. It was into this unknown country of jazz and blues that the young rebels, the myth-makers and the fact-finders of the '30s, ventured.

They kept their eyes open and looked around them, with a kind of intense, obsessive concentration. Beyond the fables and the yarn-spinning, they brought a more serious and responsible kind of creative imagination. Applying it to the dusty stock of the junkshops, the vast pile of just-discovered and completely undocumented phonograph records, castoff trivia of more popular music, they opened the doors to the unknown histories of a great American art.

Save for that inspired and obsessive teenage worrying over some dusty artifacts, all early jazz would truly *be* a legend, one as sentimentalized and as preposterously unreal as the Hollywood geniuses have always made it.

Before discography there was collecting — what in the 1930s we called "Hot Collecting." You have to collect the artifacts before you can study them. This form of junk-shopping was not only interesting and fun, but also had a certain serious importance. So it gave the name and the theme to a whole chapter in a certain important book of 1939 to which I shall refer later.

The adjective "hot" seemed natural then. As natural as the name "jazz" itself, which everyone knew was the natural name of an act that was "natural" (or at least generally so, we hoped). Much as it might enrage and affright the prudes, the adjective "hot" had already had a long and honorable history of controversy. In 1896 the subtitle to the song "Dora Dean" aroused the women's clubs of New York City the moment the sheet music hit the stands and Junior came home singing it: "Dora Dean, The Hottest Thing You Ever Seen." The club women screamed so effectively that the Post Office Department ruled the song obscene and unavailable. Its composer, Bert Williams, bowing perforce to law and order, changed "hottest" to "sweetest." The censors, God bless 'em, couldn't know that the two adjectives were far from incompatible After all, some years later, Jack Teagarden would be singing, "I like it sweet and hot." Of course, we have always known that Jackson did *not* mean coffee, nor even just music.

In fact, in 1899, as ragtime began softening up the country for the coming of jazz, a song was published with a title remarkably prophetic of the century just to come. This was Harry Mincer's piano piece called "Virginia — Two-Step and Hot Rag Swing."

So, "hot" meant something more than a desirable quality of breakfast coffee; something more, indeed, than a three-letter adjective modifying a four-letter noun. It had to do with art and with life, with a vital, compelling, soul-freeing, meaningful, musical rhythm, first called ragtime, then called jazz — a rhythm and a music truly new and revolutionary. It *was* Black Power. It *did* threaten to upset a smug musical establishment with its umbilicus still safely attached to Mother Europe.

It was unquestionably, as I once wrote, "a summons to life. This message, in the largest sense as involved in the deepest relations of an art to human life, is the real creative meaning of American jazz."

That is a long, long way from little people frightened of four-letter words like LIFE. And rummaging in second-hand stores for a Hot Five OKeh was a long, long way from mere junk collecting. And the beginnings and growth of hot discography were a long, long way from the mere glorification of the essentially trivial. For they had to do with jazz; a music so vital and persuasive, so implicatory and finally coercive, that it became, for many of its players and devotees, a way of life.

Jazz came, not from the ivory towers but from life, first from black life and then, wonder of wonders, from black *and* white life. Emerging as it did from an American stratum deprived economically and denied social, educational, esthetic, professional and moral sanctions, it was pre-daubed with prejudice, pre-judged and pre-condemned. It was, in short, just the delicious, contraband, forbidden thing to hook the teenagers of 1930.

So Jazz, then the far-out rebel cause, furnished the initial impetus to collecting records. It did not hurt, either, in those Depression days, with second-hand dealers still not wised-up to ODJB, NORK, "Jelly Roll," "Hot Fives," "New Orleans Bootblacks," and "Chicago Loopers," and anxious to get rid of old records for a nickel or a dime, so that you could get by with a half-dollar in your pocket. The day was yet far-off when a King Oliver Gennett in mint would bring ten, then twenty, then thirty dollars!

Collecting is more than mere acquisition. One dollar bill is much like another; a serial number won't make it worth ten. But a tiger maple Queen Anne highboy from New Hampshire is not the same as a Goddard mahogany one from Newport. Acquisition piles up things, collecting sorts them out. Sorting leads to classification. Classification demands study, and study reveals things like beauty, meaning, deep feeling, and unknown lives and history. Emerson paired those two: "History is properly biography."

Remember that the record industry, which is to say the music business, was not helping anyone in those days. The record labels told you nothing. The companies' specialty was to document as little as possible, get it on the market as soon as possible and, as soon as sales slowed down to a walk, lose the masters, let them deteriorate, or even destroy them.

Is this all that important? Some old foxtrot records of "Margie" for Mom to find years later in the attic and play them for little daughter? Yes, I think so. It has to do with the basically equivocal and unnatural relations of art to commerce, with the precarious position of art in a grossly materialistic culture. Why kid ourselves? Napoleon was right but he didn't go far enough. Not merely Britain, but the whole pretentious Western "Culture" — all of us — are "nations of shopkeepers."

Having bought these second-hand jazz disks of the then more or less immediate past, we young rebels did not spend riotous nights inhaling pot, doing the Watusi, and letting our hair grow. Oh, there may have been a little pot around, but it was called "tea" or "Taj." Believe it or not, we got together and listened, discussed, and argued far into the night with the neighbors yelling, "Quiet, for Chrissake!"

Discussions. Questions: Who is that playing trumpet? Trombone? Clarinet? Piano? Why doesn't this record (blue-label Columbia ten-inch number 2615-D, master number 404569) sound like Louis Armstrong when it says right here "Louis' Harlem Stompers?" Naturally Columbia would tell nobody that the band really was a new outfit of ofay cats called the Casa Loma Orchestra. Not that the Casa Loma, necessarily, stunk, but that was not the point. So, beginners that we were, we argued on: "If it says Louis, it means Louis."

"Oh, come on, *listen* will you? That band never saw Louis."

"He's right. It never even saw Harlem. That's not a Negro band at all."

Or, another night, another room, say a dormitory room in the evening, year 1934-1935. The host puts on a record.

"Bend your ears on a real oldie. It must be at least ten years old. My Dad had it and says he bought it about 1922. Now you'll hear some real old-time Negro jazz." (He plays it.)

Guest No. 1: "Scratchy as all hell. Can't you play it with a cactus needle." (Host obliges.)

Guest No. 1: "Are you kidding us? This is *Negro* jazz?"

Host: "Read the label, wise guy. 'Aunt Hagar's Children Blues,' by Ladd's Black Aces."

Guest No. 1: Wait a sec till I get a record from my room." (Goes and returns.) "O.K. spin this." (Host plays it.)

All: "It's the same record."

Guest No. 1: "Oh yeah? Here it says, 'Aunt Hagar's Children Blues' by Connorized Jazz Hounds. Bill's record is a Gennett, mine's a Connorized. Same tune, same band, but a different name and a different label."

Guest No. 2: "Hold everything. I've got a record here I just found today at the Salvation Army. Take a listen." (Plays the disk.)

All: "It's the same tune. Sounds a lot like the same band but maybe playing it at a different time."

(Wary now): "What's *that* label and what does *it* say?"

Guest No. 2: "All right. This is a Vocalion; tune, 'Aunt Hagars, etc., and the band — it says here — is Gene Fosdick's Hoosiers."

Guest No. 3: "Here's another county to hear from. Let me fetch a record from *my* room." (Goes, returns, puts his record on.)

All: "That's the same as Bob just played, Gene Somebody-or-Other's Hoosiers."

Guest No. 3: "Easy now. Same tune, same band, same performance. But this label is Beltone and it claims that the band is the Original Memphis Five."

The argument broke up at dawn with nothing settled. Correspondence began with addicts in other colleges. Who was the band? Was it Negro? Or was it white? In ensuing bashes other pertinent records were brought and compared. Records were mailed back and forth. Labels like Paramount, Puritan, Coliseum, Pathe, Triangle, Claxtonola, Chautauqua, Aco, Homochord, Grafton, Broadway, Banner, Guardsman, Scala, Davega, Perfect, Emerson, and many more began revealing duplicated tunes and takes all by one and the same band they had started with and with a real Babel of band names: Broadway Syncopators, Lanin's Southern Serenaders, Pasternacki's Orchestra, Black Diamond Serenaders, Superior Jazz Band, New Orleans Five, The Cotton Pickers, Jazz Bo's Carolina Serenaders.

In trying to outsmart the buyer, the record companies outsmarted themselves at last. An aroused generation — or a small part of it— unravelled the unutterable chicaneries and came up with some answers. It *was* one band and its real name was The Original Memphis Five. Although it was not from or related by family *or* race to Mr. Handy of Memphis. Although it wasn't all that original, it was a hell of a little band anyway, and it was a five-piece combo, even though one label lied and called it the Savannah Six.

Questions have a way of leading to more questions. These researchers, without a grant, went on and found out who the players were: trumpet, Phil Napoleon from Boston; clarinet, Jimmy Lytell from New York; that wonderful modern trombone was a little guy with spectacles from Long Island, Miff

Mole; the rhythm section was Frank Signorelli on the piano and Jack Roth on the drums.

It took a lot of discussion, a lot of correspondence (including letters the record companies never answered), and a lot of listening through murky acoustic recording and needle noise. Listening, listening, listening is what did it. A hobby became a discipline, a discipline discovered an all-but-lost cause to fight for, and the crusade found itself as an intellectual discipline married to an art.

Tin ears became sharp and discriminating. Vibrato, tone, attack, and phrasing would reveal Satchmo on an obscure record, even he had forgotten making. Or listening would tell the exact record on which he changed from cornet to trumpet. Sharper and sharper the listening: it soon could tell Louis' most accurate imitators (everyone imitated Louis) from Louis himself. A group of these cats eventually could listen to a new find, one guy fastening on trumpet, another on clarinet, and so on, and come up with the complete personnel that the companies never gave. Lists of master number sequences began to fill out, and recording dates and locations could be pinned down — bits, precious bits, of the history no one had bothered to write.

So the discipline grew. Factual distinctions led into esthetic distinctions and vice versa. The framework of a sculptor's armature began to grow and on the armature the modelling clay began to be applied. A three-dimensional topography began to appear, growing contours of a non-allegorical classic figure called History.

It was clay, it was provisional, and one day's modelling might have to be stripped off tomorrow and new clay in new contours go on instead. Did jazz really begin in 1917 with a white five called the Original Dixieland Jazz Band? What came before that? Who came before King Oliver and Freddie Keppard? Were all these guys from New Orleans?

Yes, questions lead to questions. And they led a bunch of college boys to a big, big answer at last. They discovered something big and vital at the real core of American life. All the pundits, all of the music conservatories, and nearly all of the critics, sociologists, psychologists, philosophers, and historians had missed it. It would be charitable to say that the Establishment had merely goofed.

The rebels had hit paydirt. By 1936, having spread to Europe, the discipline bore fruit in France in the first of the book-length jazz discographies, Charles Delaunay's *Hot Discography,* whose revisions and additions (with indispensable American help) went right on through the war. There was even a 1943 underground paper edition printed in Paris right under the "Ubermensch" noses.

The production of discographies has continued ever since with highly specialized and valuable ones appearing here and abroad. Some are devoted to specific styles of jazz, or the blues, others to the complete recorded oeuvre of individual artists. The discipline supports, and is supported by, special magazines like Len Kunstadt's and Bob Colton's *Record Research* and its blues offspring.

Meanwhile, in that sculptor's studio, the non-allegorical figure of Jazz History went from clay into its first bronze version. In 1939 a bunch of college boys — those rank amateurs rushing in where the Establishment angels disdained to tread — put together a book. Their names are Charles Edward Smith, Frederic Ramsey Jr., Wilder Hobson, William Russell, Stephen Smith, E. Simms Campbell, Ed Nichols, Otis Ferguson, and Roger Pryor Dodge. The title of their book, *Jazzmen,* added a new word to the language. *Jazzmen* not only was a history, it was an historical event.

It, and all the succeeding bronze figures from that suppositional studio, came from a noble kind of junk collecting called Hot Collecting that grew into Hot Discography, which, in turn, grew into the special kind of social-biographical-esthetic kind of history needed to document a true child of social forces like jazz. Having documented the otherwise soon-to-be-forgotten, *Jazzmen* helped to restore and revivify the music itself, to give the music and its players meaning, identity, and importance.

All of this is a benign revolution. I salute discography and its workers in a continuing factual discipline wedded to the greatest musical art of our century. I wish to close with a serious suggestion. It is time for the discographers of the world to translate their common bonds of interest and cooperation into an international organization. I think that the first steps toward this should be taken here today.

When that is done, I have a further suggestion which I make partly in fun, but also seriously. A great corporation has recently — and I think, blindly and callously — rejected the most famous trademark in history in favor of the mediocre and childish simplicity of a monogram. The initials RCA have now replaced the little listening dog. He is gone from the label that once gave us the ODJB, then Morton, Oliver, Goodman, the Original Memphis Five under their real name.

I think the International Discographers should adopt little "Nipper" as a symbol. He, too, is a good listener — all night *and* all day. Should we, perhaps, change the motto ever so slightly to "His Master's Number?"

NEGLECTED AREAS OF DISCOGRAPHICAL RESEARCH

A Panel Discussion

Martin Williams
Critic
Stanley Dance
Critic

Stanley Dance: I think I possibly could be the oldest discographer here because I had a hand in a book called *Rhythm on Record* by Hilton Schleman, who was a close friend of mine. Although that was an amateurish discography, it did serve a purpose at that time. Shortly afterwards, Charles Delaunay's *Hot Discography* came along and I had a hand in that too.

Having a hand in it, at that time, meant mostly taking information off the records we had. We had no idea of how far discography would go, and we had very little cooperation from the record companies. Roy Schleman was primarily a collector. He was a very good publicity agent for United Artists in London. He used to make good use of his friends. I remember that when the "Last of the Mohicans" was presented in England for the first time, a lot of budding discographers put out on a lake in London in canoes at a certain time. He pulled all kinds of stunts like that.

But he did have in his day one of the great collections because he took no notice of critics whatsoever! He simply bought what he liked. As a result, he had practically a complete collection (in England) of Jelly Roll Morton, at a time when most people regarded Jelly Roll Morton as corny. His records are still in circulation; they can usually be identified by a little tag showing the month and the year in which they were issued. For some reason Schleman attached great importance to the date of release.

What I really wanted to get to was discographical work. I prefer the term "work" to "research" because I don't regard it as a science or an art. I think it's a labor of love, and nobody makes any money out of it. I think it is, therefore, a discographer's privilege to waste his time as and if he wishes. A great many seem to concern themselves with numbers and antiquity rather than music. I was beginning to think that the '20s had been plowed over enough, until I started to do a little work at Decca and found that among the old sheets there were Vocalion records by Chick Webb. One was called *High Levee, Low Water* which I had never heard of. Rex Stewart also had several titles which had never appeared in any discography.

Owing to the shifts of the early Vocalion and Brunswick material, no plates, no tests of these records could be found; but they probably do exist somewhere, because the Decca library has been systemically rifled several times by zealous collectors who got impatient with what was happening there. However, there was one discovery which really proved that the '20s were not finished. There was a record by Edith North Johnson, issued under the name of Edith North. When I played it, one side had just a primitive blues accompaniment, but the other side was by an obviously more sophisticated pianist who played in the stride idiom. The master number was KC590 and I took it to Basie, and he said yes, that was the first record he ever made, and that it was one he had always looked for. I imagine there still are discoveries to be made in that period.

Now I am speaking primarily as a user. I have thought for a long time that it would be a great service to include composers' names in discographies. This can be very helpful and illuminating at times. From the purely technical point of view of production, I think that in discographies of, say, big bands that had made a lot of records, the full personnel should be repeated at the top of each page. It really gets difficult to keep referring to who replaced whom, and what does this little figure #4 mean; is it Frank Sinatra, or Sy Oliver singing, or what? This is obviously a refinement, but I think it is something that could be borne in mind.

Another one of my pet desires is an alphabetical index of titles. If you are researching an artist who recorded prolifically, and you are not particularly familiar with every phase of his career, you must look through pages and pages to locate a particular title. We have an index of titles in the Italian discographies of Ellington and I find these extremely useful.

In the same way, indices of sidemen would be useful. These two things could be done out of the existing discographies without trampling on anybody's rights. They could be supplementary works that anybody with the time and inclination could complete.

Another area that I think needs extensive work is the period of 78's following World War II. Some of you may think that this has been done adequately, but I do not. When I get out my magnifying glass and go through the pages of *Record Research* occasionally, I find many records that I have never heard of. I recently acquired two by Dud Bascomb; excellent records which are in no discography. I am sure that there are many more like them. More effort should be applied to that period, because even in the re-issue field some of the companies have been looking for those records. They cannot find the owners, and there is very little detail on them. If some discographers could apply themselves to that period, it would be very helpful musically, as well as rewarding from the point of view of discography.

I think that few people in America have bothered to buy Hugues Panassie's *Critical Discography.* This is an extremely valuable book, and I think more could be done in that area too. That is to say, there is a need for a discography that is not concerned with listing full personnel, but which details soloists on each performance. This is much easier to do in America than it is in Europe. However, Panassie has done it fairly accurately, primarily by talking to musicians and playing records with them.

We have come to the time when there should be more discographies of single artists. I received one recently from Belgium on Clark Terry. Clark Terry has made thousands of records already, and it would be helpful if there were other discographies of other people who made many records. Again, it is not necessary to list full personnel in books of that kind. For example, in a discography of Earl Hines, the personnel should be given for records made under his own name; but when he plays with Louis Armstrong under Armstrong's name, then it would be sufficient to list the titles and give the name of the artist.

These are some of the things that I, as a user, would find helpful. I suggest them in the hope that someone may apply himself to those areas.

Martin Williams: I can begin by flattering discographers. Hardly a day passes that I do not use the fruits of their labor. I could not function without them, and I am constantly aware of that fact.

However, I have to modify it immediately. I have used Walter Allen's *King Joe Oliver* book to the point of plagiarism. But other than that, when I say that I am using discography daily, I mean that I use Rust's volumes, Albert McCarthy's volumes, and Jepsen's volumes. It has been a long time since Blackstone was the standard reference for us all. I also use a few specialized studies, of which some, like Allen's, are invaluable. Usually, however, I am using European research, and very little American research.

What are we doing? Where is the research? With all our private publishing ventures and magazines, such as they are, where is the work? Where is the discography?

Let me make a few frivolous and, perhaps, humorous distinctions. First of all, you know it is possible to be a fake critic. To me the word "critic" has a very special meaning, and I do not use it loosely. I think there are very few critics in the world, in any field, really worthy of that name — very, very few in jazz. The field is left, by and large, to us enthusiasts and amateurs. Indeed, when a real critic comes along, the enthusiasts are apt to condemn him, attack him, ignore him, or just resent him. "It's *our* thing," they seem to say. We jazz enthusiasts press our precious music to our breasts, saying in effect, we discovered it, we love it, and who does the critic think he is to tell us what we should like? Of course, that is not really the function of critics.

I was once at a recording date featuring prominent musicians. The man who supervised the date has been involved with jazz at least since his teens. He has written reviews, he has done interviews, he has produced recordings, he has been a manager. He is, himself, an amateur musician.

On the date in question the musician was recording a solo on the 12-bar blues. His girl friend happened to walk in behind the panel glass and, as a kind of joke between them, he began making the most appalling mistakes. She smiled broadly through the glass. What he was doing was hilarious. But the man who was producing the record rushed into the studio at the end of the take, embraced the musician, and told him, quite seriously, that what he had just played was absolutely marvelous. They did not need another take on that piece. This was the one to issue. Of course, everyone there was shocked. He simply had not understood that the musician was deliberately making mistakes as a joke.

On the other hand, I read the following statement in a recent discographical magazine. It had to do with a recording which would be interesting to hear. It is a very old record and nobody has ever found a copy of it. But someone in this discographical magazine described this as one of the great undiscovered masterpieces! How could a performance that no one has heard for over 40 years or not at all, be called a masterpiece?

When I was working on a set for Victor's Vintage series — Benny Moten — I naturally used Rust's volume. Not everyone who works on that series, by the way, picks his own selections for an LP. I always have, although I have been crossed up a couple of times. I managed to talk Mike Lipskin into giving me tapes of all the Moten records made for Victor including all the alternate takes they had on hand. (I had to promise, in blood, practically, to give the tapes back to them when I got through with them!) As I began listening and referring to Rust's book, I began to notice all sorts of errors in his listing. For example, a tuba was listed when the man was playing string bass. That was one sort of mistake. Then I realized that with the vocalists, he might list a man as a singer, when it was not a man, but a woman, or a group, or there wasn't any vocal on the record. Or, there was a vocal where he had not listed one, and so forth. Then I realized that probably Rust had not heard these records, and he was probably taking the word of a lot of other people.

I began to make corrections on my pages of Rust's book. I was trying at the same time to listen to the music, and pick out the things I wanted to use on the LP. Making the corrections got to be very tiresome after a while. So I made a distinction; I said to myself: you don't like this early Moten music very much, a great deal of it you never want to hear again. This band in your opinion didn't hit its stride until after much of this stuff was recorded. So I went strictly to the job of selecting the LP. Then, when I had my selection, I went back to Rust's book and made whatever changes in my own listing for the LP that needed to be made. So there, I guess, I was functioning as a critic.

I do not mean to knock any side of the fence here — reviewers, collectors, discographers. One takes what he gets. But I have had some interesting experiences.

I teach a class in jazz at the New School. I get a strange conglomeration of students, any type you can name, including guys whose ambition is to write about rock records. (The fellow who writes about rock in *Esquire* took my course. The fruit of my labor is that he now writes about rock and attacks jazz!) But I get a number of collectors, my age and older, in this course and they are, to me, among the most interesting students. A number of them have held on to some of the same records I use in class since they were teenagers, but they haven't really listened to them. I mean it — not so that they know what is going on. I have put the simplest outline of what happens on a recording, chorus by chorus, on the blackboard, and then played the record in question. It might be a record that has been in a man's collection all his life, but he jumps up and down with delight. He say, "Oh yes, yes, *that's* it." It is so exciting to him. He probably knows every note by heart. Yet, until then, he hadn't really listened. From one point of view, of course, it's quite exciting when such a thing happens. And yet is a way it is upsetting, for he has not really *heard* the music he loves.

Now let me draw a parallel in another field: comic strips. It is handy enough for me because of a kind of semi-active interest I have in other so-called popular arts. You may not know it, but there are lots of people out there who are nuts about comic strips, who dig up old comic strips, collect, buy, sell, and trade them. They have their own publications, most of them mimeographed. (They are not in our class yet! They seldom use offset!) I can promise you that the level of scholarship and criticism in that field is remarkably high; you do not find very much wasted time or effort.

I received recently a little critical folder by a man living in San Francisco, named Bill Blackbeard. In the field of comics and drawings he is a remarkable man. I was unacquainted with him until I got this publication. But when I read it, I realized that he knows, for example, what is involved in drawing a picture, designing a page, or designing a daily strip.

His scholarship is amazing. For example, someone recently revived, in a comic book, that marvelous old newspaper strip called "Polly and her Pals" — there was really original drawing style and comic attitude in that thing. Bill Blackbeard's knowledge was so good that he knew that it was taken from the Sunday strips of such and such a date, of such and such a year. He went over to his collection, looked it up, and verified it, just like that.

Yet, with all of this knowledge and scholarship, this man Blackbeard is an excellent critic. He makes the finest critical distinctions on the highest level. He knows *why* and *how* something is good or not so good. Those are really the critic's questions, *how* and *why* something is good. Blackbeard also has impeccable taste. Anything he likes, I want to see.

I wish we had a man like that in jazz. I wish we had a man who was an expert discographer, a good listener, a good scholar, and a good critic. We have never had such a person.

However, if you become a little more critically aware of the music, I think it will help you, and help us all. Of course, we are all going to make mistakes. But I think that we should know when we hear a tuba; we should know when there are two trumpets on a record instead of one; we should hear the music chorus by chorus; we should know the 12-bar blues when we hear it or the two most common 16-bar outlines when we hear them.

We should even know the "I Got Rhythm" changes when musicians are using them — they are the most common chord changes used in jazz after the blues. In a recent issue of a discographical magazine a man was making a list of related pieces and under "I Got Rhythm" he listed one piece! There are thousands of "I Got Rhythm" pieces, thousands of them, a new one every other day.

Well, I'm not trying to make a musicologist out of anybody — I can't because I'm not equipped to. But it will help you to learn to listen better. You may know you have made an error in the number of instruments on a record — you will know that, and it will not hurt you to know. Read the few critics that there are. Don't believe them. Don't take what they say on faith. Don't take up a banner for this one or that one. But ask yourselves, "Why is this man saying this? Why does he believe this about this musician? What does he say about this other musician? Do I agree? Why?"

Ask yourself also, "Do I *know* what a tuba sounds like on an old accoustical record? Or is that a bass saxophone? Do I know the difference in the sound of the instruments?" These are not esoteric questions and asking them is not going to turn you into a musician. They are ordinary, common, everyday questions, or should be, for all of us. It is fun too, by the way. It is a great way to listen to music, I promise you — maybe the only way.

I second Stanley Dance's motion for more research on the post-World War II records. There are a lot of companies working on reissuing those records and they need that kind of information.

I also emphatically second the motion for composer credit in any regular comprehensive discography. I need that kind of data every day. For example, I had a set-to with Mr. Allen last month, and if we both had known composer credit on the pieces involved the whole problem would have been cleared up in a minute.

I would like to come back to the question of specialized discography and comment on a specific one. I have said that criticism would help us all, that some kind of critical knowledge, or just ordinary musical knowledge of an elementary sort would help us all. But the specialized discography on Benny Goodman is a good example of how not to use a kind of critical commentary in discography, in my opinion. It is very useful book to me, factually. But critically, it seems to me rather an adolescent volume. The author gushingly embraces Benny Goodman in the same terms he did when he was a teenager; he sounds as if he is terribly infatuated with Benny Goodman's music. From his tone, he might also be Benny Goodman's press agent. And that kind of quasi-criticism is not very useful in such a specialized study. It is a subjective confession of a love affair that should have been laid to rest at age 20 in my opinion. However, there *are* many critical things to say about Benny Goodman. And they need saying.

NEGLECTED AREAS OF RESEARCH

A Panel Discussion

The Panel on Neglected Areas led to a prolonged discussion by the audience and panelists on a variety of points. The following is a summary of the major areas of concern.

First, many participants felt that discographers should indicate the sources of their data (e.g., label, company files, participating musician, personal opinion based on listening, etc.). Without full attribution of sources, discography is not scientific research. Errors are perpetuated. And subsequent researchers repeat the effort of going to the same sources for the same data.

On the other hand, there is a problem of space. The multiplicity of sources used by discographers would probably make the book unmanageable if fully cited. Discographers may be less scientific researchers than dogged compilers from numerous sources. However, abbreviations and symbols could provide source material without excessive use of space. And some source indication is particularly vital for rare or obscure material not readily available to the discography's users.

Second, much of the problem of accuracy in listings and the resultant demand for source references might be lessened if there were greater emphasis on specialized monographs on individual performers or schools. The specialized monograph does not have the same constraints of space as the massive comprehensive work. The specialist can check sources more carefully, and he will be listening to most of the records involved, a task which is impossible for the comprehensive discographer.

The Institute of Jazz Studies, or some consortium of jazz organizations, could seek a grant to pull together such specialized efforts into an encyclopedia, guided by advisory committees to handle specific technical problems.

Third, an alternative approach to either comprehensive efforts or specialized monographs would be an international circulation of simple data sheets, possibly constituting a loose-leaf mimeographed discography. A formal system would replace random personal exchanges and articles in obscure magazines. The loose-leaf compilation, easily corrected and added to, would be preferable to large printed volumes, presumably comprehensive but actually riddled by errors and omissions.

Other participants, however, noted that publication of a comprehensive work permits all authorities around the world to focus on correction and change, which would never occur through a haphazard exchange of loose sheets. Imperfect but comprehensive discographies are a "bird in the hand," especially valuable to persons distant from archives and source materials. If even 60 percent of the material is universally available, everyone can contribute to correction and addition.

Given the existence of these comprehensive volumes, the next step might be the formation of a board of discographers, each taking one or more specialized areas and jointly producing an annual volume of corrections and additions to Rust, Jepsen, and others. Such an annual supplement would be far cheaper and quicker to produce than a reprinting of the original works with new material.

Fourth, technical improvements in the production of discographies might solve some of the problems. Most discographies, for example, are typographically poor. A creative use of typography would improve their usefulness as reference books and make it easier to indicate sources, doubtful data, and the like, without excessive use of space. Even more radical would be the use of computer technology in compiling material and in storing it centrally. The University of Colorado has begun programming information on the music of Duke Ellington.

Fifth, another vexing problem is the tendency of discographers to make critical judgements which limit the value of their books to anyone not sharing those judgements. For example, in deciding what is jazz, they may omit some recordings of dance bands with jazz soloists, leaving the reader with an incomplete view of the band's recordings.

ARMED FORCES TRANSCRIPTIONS AS SOURCE MATERIALS

Jerry Valburn
Audio Engineer, Collector, and Author

I hope to give you some serious thoughts about the problems of cataloguing and documenting information about transcriptions.

The transcription is generally a 16-inch disc, which cannot be played on conventional 12-inch turntables at home. Some of us have cherished our old equipment or bought some from radio stations. The stations no longer use them, but prior to the long-playing record the 16-inch records were the only ones that contained 15 minutes of programming material per side. They were cut standard groove.

As far as I can discover the first transcriptions were made about 11 or 12 years after the first jazz records of the ODJB. While Rudi Blesh and Charles Edward Smith were looking through junk shops, the New York studios of some major recording companies were setting aside a special series of master numbers and transcriptions were being custom-made for advertisers. They used personalities and studio bands, and these recordings were played on radio stations around the country.

Before the introduction of acetate in the middle '30s, which made instantaneous cuts possible, all 78 records were etched in wax and then processed. These transcription records were cut on 16-inch waxes and then were processed and pressed on a very heavy shellac. In the early '30s they developed a plastic type of compound which was similar to, but not quite as quiet as, the vinyl that was introduced in the later '30s by broadcasting transcriptions.

One transcription, made for the Meadows Washing Machine Company in Illinois, contained the usual commercial but followed it with the tune, "Angry," by Ray Miller. Many of you may remember that Ray Miller made a version of "Angry" for Brunswick, featuring Muggsy Spanier.

Two interesting points about the recordings are the superiority of the performance on the transcription, which was made for use by radio stations only, and the merit of a transcription as opposed to a 78, because of the length of playing time.

During the '30s all the recording companies had their own transcription divisions and they made special, customized cuts, longer than the standard records. Stations around the country could pay a small royalty and play programs which featured all the big bands, including Basie, Ellington, Lunceford, and the famous Rhythm Makers Series on RCA Thesaurus of Benny Goodman, Charlie Barnet, Bunny Berigan, and Artie Shaw.

Most of these have been annotated in a discography, now out of print, called *Transcography.* I understand that Ken Crawford of Pittsburgh, an authority on these particular transcriptions, is planning a revised edition.

Now we come to World War II and some major problems. The government had set up the Office of Special Services within the War Department to supply entertainment for the troops. In 1942 our troops were scattered from the Aleutians to South America, from England to North Africa and all over the Pacific. To reach this far-flung audience, the Armed Forces Radio Service (AFRS) was established and became what is probably the largest single record operation anywhere in the world. Studios and facilities were set up in New York and Hollywood to get direct lines in from the major networks. They recorded every single program that the GI wanted to hear, including comedy by Jack Benny, Fred Allen, Fibber McGee and Molly, Bob Hope, and Red Skelton. Every one of these artists had a series of AFRS and would cut a master, make 16-inch pressings, and send these pressings to all the AFRS radio stations around the world. To this day its successor, AFRTS (Armed Forces Radio and Television Service), is still in existence, playing tapes, of course, instead of records.

This extensive operation was great for a number of reasons. First, you may recall that in July 1942, Mr. Petrillo and the AFM put a ban on commercial recording, and, although the music went on, musicians were not allowed to record. They made guest appearances on radio shows, though, and those that were recorded by AFRS are the only ones around. At that time, 16-inch blank acetate discs were hard to come by because their base is metal and, during the war, the only discs available for commercial use had a glass base. Unfortunately, they were not durable and most were broken or destroyed. However, the AFRS could obtain 16-inch acetates for their pressings.

This operation is not to be confused with the V-disc. The V-disc was a separate government program whereby artists donated their time and services to make 12-inch 78 recordings that were sent to bases around the world and played on portable phonographs by the GIs themselves. The 16-inch AFRS records were made the same way as commercial transcriptions, and were broadcast over various Armed Forces Stations.

Now comes the most interesting and important part. In addition to recording the great radio show series, and we will confine ourselves to those that are related to jazz, AFRS also originated their own programs. They used the best musical talent available as well as the best production and programming brains that had been drafted into the services. They started a series of shows in late 1942 that ran through World War II and continued thereafter.

Of these shows, the first and biggest was a weekly series called *Command Performance,* most of which originated in Hollywood. The top movie stars and personalities performed on and emceed these shows. They consisted of a mixture of everything from hillbilly to jazz and comedy routines. An early 1943 *Command Performance* show included one of the few live performances of Thomas "Fats" Waller with Dinah Shore as the mistress of ceremonies. The Waller segment featured "Your Feet's Too Big" and "Handful of Keys."

Incidentally, although the signoff for the show was "Until it's over, Over There," *Command Performance* stayed on the air until 1950, the slogan urging all our hospitalized boys back to their home from over there.

The most important series in my opinion was one that happily gave preference to the music of the Negro. This was called *Jubilee,* and was on the air from the fall of 1942 through 1950. The first program featured Duke Ellington and Ethel Waters. Until this time, the Negro had not been given proper exposure on radio networks, except for guest appearances: it was always the white bands that got the commercial shows. But here was a show aimed primarily at the Negro GI and all other people who liked hot licks, presided over by a fat, cherubic emcee named Ernie "Bubbles" Whitman who had been a Negro performer in comedy before the war.

For this series of programs they went on location with recording equipment, or before a live audience, and took down complete segments by all the great Negro artists. Then in the control rooms in Hollywood, where Allied records were cut, they put these shows together. It is quite remarkable when you realize that this was an era when tape did not exist. All the mixing and splicing had to be done perfectly, from disc to disc. Here are some of the artists who appeared on over four hundred different half-hour *Jubilee* programs: Duke Ellington, Count Basie, Jimmy Lunceford, Benny Carter, Fletcher Henderson, Cab Calloway, Noble Sissle, Claude Hopkins, Andy Kirk, Lionel Hampton, Cootie Williams, Harlan Leonard, Jay McShann, Teddy Wilson, Billy Eckstine, Earl Hines, Benny Goodman, Boyd Raeburn, Louis Armstrong, Jimmy Mundy, Ike Carpenter, Earl Spencer, Coleman Hawkins, Eddie Heywood, Roy Eldridge, Charlie Barnet, Jack Teagarden, Jack McVea, Lucky Millinder, Gerald Wilson, Lester Young, Al Killian, and Howard McGhee.

They also included some of the earliest bop performances by Charlie Parker and Bud Powell with Cootie Williams, and also Howard McGhee's early bop sextet on the West Coast. Since the series continued until after World War II, the newly modern bands of Woody Herman, Stan Kenton, and others also recorded live performances on *Jubilee.*

I went through my *Jubilee* shows and picked one that I happen to like very much; a segment called The All-Star Sextet, consisting of Vic Dickenson, Willie Smith, Les Paul (of all people), Eddie Heywood, and Sid Catlett — all jamming together. *Jubilee* would bring in different musicians and throw them together. Sometimes it was just great, other times it didn't work, but here they are doing "I Found a New Baby." (Recording is played.)

The quality of the Armed Forces recordings was excellent, even by today's standards. They were not stereo, but they captured the heart of jazz and of big band swing — things that would have been forever lost if they had not been taken down by AFRS.

AFRS used two major programs that were taken right from commercial radio. One of the most successful shows in radio, geared to jazz and swing enthusiasts, was a commercial show by the Coca Cola Company called *Spotlight Bands.* AFRS took this show down each day and from it made up 15-minute transcriptions which they also called *Spotlight Bands.* Here is one from Jefferson Barracks, Missouri, called "Jeep Rhythm," recorded by Jimmy Lunceford in 1945. (Record is played.)

The other two most important radio series in 1944, 1945, and 1946 that relate directly to jazz were those of Duke Ellington and Eddie Condon. Ellington went on the air for the Treasury Department over ABC in 1945 and 1946, and from this, AFRS made a series of seventy-eight different transcriptions. Details of these transcriptions will be in my book and also in the *Discographer.*

The Eddie Condon concert series were forty-eight live broadcasts by ABC from Town Hall in New York City, and later from the studios at Radio City. The beautiful thing about these programs is that Eddie had many distinguished Negro guests such as Sidney Bechet, "Hot Lips" Page, Earl Hines, and others in addition to his Dixieland Stalwarts. Here is part of one show with the Condon mob doing "Royal Garden Blues." (Record is played.)

In addition to all of these, AFRS had many other jazz series, some of which started, ironically, after World War II. Quite a few of these, of course, were not heard by servicemen in action but were enjoyed by patients in the hospials. On the West Coast an entire series, called *Just Jazz* and devoted mainly to progressive jazz, was started by Gene Norman. Another series, called *Downbeat,* that went on during World War II and thereafter, featured candid interviews with top musicians and played live performances by the band. Probably the most affectionately remembered of all the AFRS series had a beautiful title, *One Night Stand.* As the title says, it was a dance band remote and here the Armed Forces had no equal. With radio lines available to them every night of the week, they went to the Savoy Ballroom, to the West Coast to Southgate or the Trianon, to Chicago, St. Louis, etc. Bands that had never had nationwide exposure on radio were heard over AFRS.

The quality is beautiful, the only difference from the commercial broadcast is an Armed Forces opening and close. So we have Tiny Bradshaw, Charlie

Parker, Dizzy Gillespie, Claude Hopkins, Lionel Hampton, and others, as well as all the new modern groups like Boyd Raeburn. Most people enjoy the Woody Herman band of 1944 and here is *One Night Stand* No. 365, originally a CBS broadcast, and a tune Woody did called "The 125th Street Prophet." (Record is played.)

I have mentioned just a few of the series of AFRS. At one point during the war it was turning out approximately seven hundred different transcriptions every week, and each show was part of a numbered series, whether it was Kate Smith, James Melton, the NBC *Symphony of the Air*, the Philharmonic, soap opera, Dunninger, or *Can You Top This*. Changes were only made when a show had a commercial in the title: *Kraft Music Hall*, with Bing Crosby, was changed to *Music Hall; Chamber Music Society of Lower Basin Street* became *Basin Street; Fitch Band Wagon* became *Band Wagon*.

At the end of World War II most of this material was scheduled to be destroyed. A carte blanche copyright had been granted AFRS to use this material for their own purposes, but no royalties had ever been paid to the performers. Quite a bit of it was actually destroyed, but the remainder of the material was turned over to veterans hospitals, to be played on the bedside network, and to the Library of Congress. In addition, there were many collectors among the GI's and a great many of these records have filtered home. They remain, historically speaking, our one link with the '40s and the great music that was produced during those years.

I am sorry that Rudi Blesh's great series of jazz shows, *This Is Jazz*, was never recorded by AFRS because they were active at that time. However, they thought enough of Mr. Blesh and the name of the show to use the title on a series of transcriptions made at the Playboy Jazz Festival in 1960 in Chicago.

Today, on Armed Forces Network, as it is now called, you could be listening to an Ellington sacred concert or one of the few weekly pick-ups that CBS makes from the Riverboat in New York City. These shows and the commercial radio shows that are done on the air are still played on our networks for our service men around the world. We will always be thankful to Uncle Sam and to Armed Forces Radio for what they have left us. Our big problem now is to annotate all this material, determine personnels and dates, identify composers and arrangers, and find out something about the bands that never made commercial records but played so well on these transcriptions. It is a big field but one that should be researched by collectors seriously interested in the big band music and small group jazz of that time.

Unfortunately, the discographical information gathered by the government was very slight. They put out file cards after the war, the Library of Congress went after them — but most of the early cards and information on those were thrown out.

For example on the Ellington records I used for my book, I actually had to go back to acetates of the commercial broadcasts and script the announcer's introduction to the tunes, time them, and then go to the Armed Forces disc and play them against the commercial broadcasts to positively identify that it came from that particular program source. It was quite a job.

One last thing: anybody who collects this type of material should get in touch with me because I'm starting to collate additional work on my own book. Some day we might at least have a working catalog of what does exist on these AFRS transcriptions. Although I thought I was pretty well versed in all the series, I received a letter from Charles Delaunay about two months ago asking if I had these Kid Ory Shows in my collection, and he listed 26 different Kid Ory shows I don't even know about. Now I'm waiting to get them from France. So you see, this area should not be neglected.

ARCHIVAL PRACTICES OF THE RECORDING COMPANIES — I

Frank Driggs
Free-lance producer and jazz historian

Columbia Records has been pretty active in reissuing a fair amount of their archive material since before World War II. John Hammond started the Red Label Series in 1940, reissuing a lot of records that came out in the '20s and '30s, and later George Avakian continued reissuing when LP's first came out. He did the memorable four-album set on Bessie Smith, four albums on Louis Armstrong, three on Bix Beiderbecke, and a few other individual LP's. He stopped reissuing records, for the most part, when he started recording people like Dave Brubeck.

When I came in, in 1960, John Hammond had just returned to Columbia from Vanguard Records, ostensibly to head a major reissue program, since there had been such a long hiatus since the last things Avakian had done. John is not the kind of man to sit in one type of position very long, so he immediately got himself involved in a tremendous number of recording projects, and got me into work on the reissue program.

The first project was one of my favorites, Fletcher Henderson. I spent the entire summer of 1960 doing research and making an arrangement with a well-known record dealer, Jake Schneider.

Columbia had an arrangement with him whereby we could borrow, from his enormous collection, any records that we did not have masters of (a goodly percentage of anything in the '20s and '30s). We were able to borrow about 80 percent of the material that we needed.

Of course, there are many other collectors in this area who have been very helpful in lending me things. Columbia had had a strong sense of public responsibility for making a large part of their old catalog available. Now most collectors will say it was not enough.

As the man who produced it, I know that it was not enough, but from about 1960 to 1965 we produced quite a bit. I have had arguments and lengthy correspondence with collectors all over the world about why I made the choices I did for reissue. My reply was that, at that time, I thought that a certain artist was a particularly good person to reissue, or that the New Orleans, Chicago, Harlem Anthology series seemed a particularly valid concept.

At that time Columbia seemed to be committed to doing things in multi-record packages with lavishly printed booklets. This started in 1961 with the *Thesaurus of Classic Jazz,* basically a Red Nichols-Miff Mole anthology that included Bix Beiderbecke, Tommy Dorsey, Eddie Lang and most of the other white musicians of the late '20s. That one, incidently, was produced by Dick DuPage who is no longer in the music business. I worked on it to the extent that I re-wrote DuPage's program notes which were, perhaps, not as commercial as they might have been. Then I worked on the sets of Fletcher Henderson, Billie Holiday, Joe Venuti, Eddie Lang, Woody Herman, Duke Ellington, Jack Teagarden, Swing Street, and several blues people.

Columbia believed that if you put out a single LP on a jazz artist, unless it was Basie, Ellington, or Billie Holiday, it would not catch enough public attention. They thought that multi-record sets would; so they spent a lot on those boxes and booklets. I would say that in the beginning they paid off. Certainly the Fletcher Henderson, the *Thesaurus,* the Billie Holiday, and, I guess one or two after that, probably made money.

However, once the public is used to one kind of product, after a while they take it for granted, and I think this is what happened. There is no one way to please the tastes of record collectors all over the world. Billie Holiday would be loved by many and hated by just as many, so you try to pick things that you think are valid. Columbia had been pretty successful in maintaining that policy until about a year ago, then they tended to draw in their horns.

Their policy as far as maintaining their archives is concerned, has been very much up and down over the years. During the '30s Columbia Records was owned by the American Record Company and was just a label which was discontinued entirely between 1936 and 1939. They were destroying masters even that far back. At one point, during the war, the scrap metal drive consumed about a hundred thousand masters from Columbia alone. That many more from Victor and probably from Decca were lost as well. Nobody will ever know because that kind of correspondence, if it still exists, is under lock and key.

The reasons for this being done were patriotic at the time, although not selective in terms of what was valuable as musical Americana. Polish, Ukraiian, and hundreds of Chinese language records were saved, but Duke Ellingtons and Louis Armstrongs are missing. I could not begin to list records that we know are important musically but have not existed for 30 years. As recently as 1962, records were still being destroyed.

Some were not Columbia's property: they had had in storage a number of 16-inch transcriptions that were made for film companies, and sound tracks and advertising that had been made for obscure independent companies which were then chucked out. They had, for example, the sound track of Josephine Baker's movie *Siren of the Tropics* which I desperately wanted to hear because it had a fairly good band, and which would have been an interesting document to keep because it was so obscure. I bet there's not one person in this room who ever saw that film. This kind of thing was being thrown out as late as 1963.

Fortunately, John Hammond, myself, and a few other concerned individuals were able to stop it, but by that time the damage had been done. However, there were discoveries that offset the losses. I found those rare Jabbo Smith recordings from 1935 that I subsequently used in smaller anthologies, and other things that had not been listed or had been considered lost. There were many alternate takes and things like that, some of which were subsequently used.

As you know, there are perhaps 3,000 to 5,000 collectors throughout the world who will buy everything that you put out. But, 5,000 records is not considered much of a record sale by a company the size of Columbia — and without giving any trade secrets away, many times we didn't even sell 5,000 copies. The same thing is true with Victor and Decca. Each has different standards of merchandising and they had possibly realized at the start that these records would not be major sellers to compete with Dave Brubeck, Erroll Garner, or another such commercial artist.

A woman named Helene Chmura was in archives for many years. She was possibly the most cooperative person because she answered just about every request for information that came through. She was kind enough to mimeograph and make up lists of most of the matrix and catalogue series of recordings that had been made by the company or its predecessors. She started something which probably will never be finished, but these lists are now in the hands of maybe a dozen of the serious researchers in this room. It's a good thing these things were done because she happened to have a particular dedication that went above and beyond her job. When Columbia moved from 799 Seventh Avenue to 52nd Street, her job was expanded and she was given charge of another department concerned with the daily schedules of singles, albums, taped products, and all the stereo things. She could not keep her interest in the old records, which was what she really loved, so she resigned.

Since that time we have had several different people running the archives. Most of them have been pretty good; as long as I was there as a regular employee I used to see all the letters that came in, and I would help answer them, if not actually do some of the work myself. I would tell them what to send out and they answered many of the requests. They still do, since the woman in charge of the archives now is quite cooperative. Columbia does request that if the information from Columbia is published in a book or magazine that Columbia should get a copy.

I would say that Columbia's policy for reissuing records now is somewhat in limbo. The only thing I have currently on tap is a four-record blues anthology going back to the box again. I have been putting out a few single records on Epic — both labels are owned by CBS. Reissuing jazz has all but stopped now because I think they believe that they have no way of selling these records. I have to agree, because there are just not enough retail outlets in the United States that will carry monaural records. How to solve this I don't know.

I am also issuing a number of albums over at CBS in England. Three albums came out late last year (1968) and there are others that are due soon. For example, we produced a Chick Webb album in England and also one in the United States. It only had 12 titles, for reasons that I will not go into here. I re-mastered the whole album when we discovered a piece of equipment that was designed to help make phony stereo. It happened to clean up the sound very well on any 78 record. I sent the whole thing over to England with 16 titles instead of 12 and they produced it. Consequently, it is a better bargain to get these from England.

England is going ahead with a policy of issuing single LP's. I am producing them all and there will be perhaps six or eight in any given year, for the next two or three years. I cannot tell you what order they will appear in, but I have sent over nine LP's and three have been issued so far. Rex Stewart's and Bukka White's albums are coming up, with several other things. At least they are maintaining a serious interest and they sell as many in England as we do here in the United States; and England is about the size of Pennsylvania. This is the situation you face, how do you market these things in the United States?

Although there is actually a CBS label which is an aegis for issuing records internationally, the company here looks at it from the standpoint of physical storage space. For them to take up warehouse space with an LP that is only going to sell 5,000 copies just does not pay. They are dealing with albums that sell over 25,000 and, in terms of the kind of business they do, they are right. Aesthically it may be wrong, but in business your stockholders demand that your profits get larger and larger every year.

One possible solution is to develop a consortium of university presses to issue non-commercial or specialty material which either is not produced in this country or has been cut out of the catalog. This idea has not received much acceptance yet, but some solution will have to be reached because there is a lot of material that is public record now and should be available.

ARCHIVAL PRACTICES OF THE RECORDING COMPANIES — II

Orrin Keepnews
Milestone Records

My first experience in the record business was, as it happens, my only experience with a major label reissue and has a direct bearing on just this problem. The late Bill Grauer and I were involved in the Label X 10-inch reissue series of the early '50s. That came about as a result of a wonderful example of a lack — not only of archival procedure, but even of archival knowledge — on the part of RCA Victor.

In those days they were so damned ignorant of what they had in their possession that a famous bootleg label with the rather revealing name of "Jolly Roger" had its pressings made by the custom pressing department of RCA Victor. When there were two albums made up entirely of Victor and one album of Columbia material being pressed for the bootlegger at RCA Victor, there was a tremendous expose. This was revealed with copies of invoices and other evidence by the *Record Changer Magazine* which Bill and I were then publishing. Suddenly there was a startled reaction from the powers at RCA Victor. They were astonished when we said in our expose, "What kind of custodians of a public trust are these that they not only allowed somebody to steal this material from them but they are making a profit by holding the highwayman's horse." They were also startled when we made the point that the so-called bootleggers were pretty much people who got sick and tired of not getting answers to their letters to the Victors and the Columbias of the world, and had gone off on their own tangent. I must say this about the power of the press — we were contacted by RCA Victor as a result of this expose. It was my first direct involvement in the record business and I thought it was easy to be in touch with people at the major labels about discographical and reissue problems; I later discovered that was an illusion!

But they contacted us, assuming that we were doing this because we were interested in issuing records ourselves. The fact is that we did not have any such interest. Both Bill and I were putting out *The Record Changer* as a sideline, while working at other things. Actually, as it developed, RCA Victor inadvertently put me in the record business. I do not know whether I want to thank them for it or not, after all these years.

They assumed that we wanted to issue records because we had mentioned all the people who had tried unsuccessfully to get reissue projects started with them. For quite some time we were in very serious discussions with people at RCA Victor about leasing material to us. As a matter of fact, that really is how Riverside Records came into existence. When RCA told us that they were going to give us a lot of Victor records to reissue, we decided we might as well have a record label to put them on. After about six months of conversation, somebody developed cold feet about allowing this material, which they had done nothing with for years, to pass out of RCA's control into the hands of someone else. What it boiled down to, I think, was really a corporate fear of the company divesting itself of control over its own property regardless of the fact that it wasn't going to do anything with it anyway. They then shifted to "Well, instead of our giving it to you, why don't you produce this material for us." which we did.

What makes that corporate point of view logical is that it immediately made this project become something very practical. In its inception this had nothing to do with "Label X," a new subsidiary they were about to launch. The whole theory, from their point of view, was that somebody would be putting out a lot of albums and everybody knows that a new label can use a lot of material to start with, and here was a ready-made series of albums that they could have.

They attempted to merchandise it as if it were standard material. We knew that the standard distribution procedures of a major label would be a pretty deadly way to try to sell a series of jazz reissues. We believed that it could be much more successful going to the stores that the collectors go to. The basic point I'm making is that one can talk theory all one wants, but the life or death of a reissue series on a major label is totally dependent on whether or not it makes enough money. I'm injecting a pessimistic note of practicality about all these wonderful projects. I am convinced, in advance, that any major label will, at the last minute, balk at letting its stuff get away.

Since my Label X experience, I have been entirely involved with the reissuing of material gathered from a variety of independent sources. I have probably done more with material from Paramount than from anywhere else, although Riverside had the Gennett material, and for a while, the Circle material of Rudi Blesh. With Rudi's material we at least had the mothers and the masters, but with Paramount Records there are no archives because they were destroyed in a big fire way back before any of us were involved. We must now rely on the good graces of collectors, as well as on digging out source material ourselves. With Gennett there were a certain number of mothers, but there must be an evil genii who handled that matter because when Riverside bought Gennett, when the metal parts arrived, we found that most of them were Polish language records, '20s pop records, and about three King Olivers.

The whole problem with ancient material from independent sources is that you literally have to create your own archives. Everyone knows what that means because the records you want are always in unbearably bad condition. Fortunately, a number of valuable processes have been developed for putting these records in shape. We can thank God that recording processes in those days were so bad that there are no "highs" on these records to begin with. Now, when you cut off the highs to get rid of surface noise, you really change very little.

I am on my second go-round with much of this material. That is, I am putting out records on Milestone that include material reissued on Riverside. Those ancient Paramount records are now 15 years older than when I approached them for the first time, and correspondingly worse; even tapes made years ago, when available, have not been very well cared for during the last ten years. I found strangely that my best source material is often an unplayed copy of a 10-inch reissued LP that I put out years ago.

For example, Riverside, in its early days, had a leasing deal with English Decca and many 10-inch Riversides appeared on the London label. They fooled around with the master tapes we sent them and, as often happens, they improved them. The Londons were better in quality, in some respects, than the Riversides.

They had the guts to echo them a little bit (which we thought was a great impurity) and, I think, this enhanced them. In putting out a Ma Rainey album on Milestone, quite recently, I used a 10-inch London LP as my source material for about half of the titles. And I treated it as source material, which is the only thing you can do.

In other words, I should not care whether this London LP is the original, sacred, 78, shellac Paramount or whether it is a reissue. It can be reprocessed, treated, have its noises removed, and, perhaps, certain of its hidden qualities dragged out. We worked with it and put it out. An enthusiastic, rather knowledgeable, former British journalist, who is now in this country, paid me an immense compliment without realizing it. He said he was so happy that this was available because it was such an improvement on his only other source of this material — a 10-inch London LP.

There is an important lesson in archival practice for all of us to learn from this: that there really is nothing sacred and the music and the content of the record is what is important.

The archival and discographical problems of these items are rather awesome because a little knowledge is a dangerous thing. We had the Gennett ledgers and recording cards, and there is a lot of very interesting information on them. I do not know how they did it, but the British discographers were always right about which Paramount records really were recorded in the Gennett studies, and things like that. Those cards contain the same kinds of information that I know exist, at least, at Victor. We discovered at Victor that the sheets that they had were primarily engineering information sheets; and no one anticipated the existence of discographers and collectors. Therefore, these cards contain a great deal on the instrumentation, for example. I cannot think of anything more frustrating than to find on a card for some record where there is controversy about the personnel, that there were two cornets, one trombone, two saxophones, and the appropriate rhythm, and, from there on it is guesswork. In the case of Paramount, there is nothing. I think the worst thing is to have a little information, perhaps only enough to let you know that the discographies are wrong, but not enough to let you make brilliant improvements on them.

Another problem is that the average discographer/collector lacks the point of view of the professional record person, like Frank Driggs or Stanley Dance. We live and work in the atmosphere of the record business as well as with our personal and professional enthusiasms and interests. A lot of practicalities of the record business get to be second nature to us. For instance, in the Gennett ledgers, there are lots of confusing recording dates that were sometimes just a few days apart. I know of instances in which you could infer from the most authoritative source, the Gennett pages themselves, that something was recorded on a specific date. However, the date they were using was the date on which the material went to the plating plant and the mother was created. It was usually within a week of the recording date, but it was not the recording date. If you know something about the record business and know that the metal parts are what records get made from, you can understand that.

One of my pet gripes since being involved with recordings is about those cases in which it is reputed that "so-and-so is on that record because he told me so himself." I know from personal experience in the record business that he really has no reason to remember. He may have made fifty dates with almost the same personnel that you are asking him about.

There are certain kinds of information that you are not going to get first-hand from the guy who was there, because quite apart from whether he remembers or not, he'll give you the answer that he knows you want to have. That is the first argument against taking the word of a musician: he wants to be nice to you. And there is no reason why you should remember where you were on the night of January 16. So, why should he recall a similar situation?

Currently at Milestone we are getting ready to analyze all the old Eddie Condon broadcasts. We have made arrangements with Condon to do this the way the American Federation of Musicians insists it should be done. If someone wants to use as a recording anything that comes into existence as something other than a commercial recording, the musicians involved must be paid at current union scale. There is a lot of difference between 1944 scale and 1969 scale. It's going to be very complicated. We will have to wait until we pick our material, then we will figure out who is entitled to what kind of money. The basic point is that you must legitimatize this stuff as records, literally by acting as if you were making a record date with Mr. Condon as the leader, which was his role when the broadcasts were originally recorded.

By and large there is more rarity and uniqueness to those Condons than to, let's say, a Jimmy Lunceford transcription because there is a lot of Jimmy Lunceford on record.

In the case of Condon, there is a limited number of men involved so it is like paying for a medium-size record date. We are not about, if the opportunity presents itself, to pay for a big band date. When you handle material that was created for phonograph records in the first place, the musicians have been properly paid (except in the case of the leader's artist royalty), but with the Condon broadcasts it is, in effect, creating records for the first time from an administrative and financial standpoint.

Let me make another interesting point. From time to time, the jazz-collecting fraternity is the unintended beneficiary of activities in other areas of the record market. Right now, certain types of blues are very popular. It has nothing to do with us and our tastes, except coincidentally. Now Blind Lemon Jefferson is a country blues singer of considerable popularity among young blues enthusiasts, and, on a practical basis, his material on Milestone (a much smaller enterprise than Riverside was) is selling considerably better than similar material sold on Riverside ten years ago. That same set of circumstances will make Columbia reissue a blues artist today whom they would not have considered reissuing five years ago.

I'm not terribly worried about the stereo-mono thing. I am prepared to issue the records the way God intended them to be and, actually, I also think it behooves any of us who are dealing with material that is already forty years old to be a little patient and take a long view. The chances are that if we give the silly record industry another six months or a year, they will be able to forget that there ever was this particular problem.

The problem came about because there was tremendous duplication; all new recordings were coming out both mono and stereo. Finally, at the wholesale and retail end, they balked at this duplication and came to a single standard. The obvious next step has been delayed by the fact that the world is full of bargains; you can get all the monaural records at $1.50 and this makes monaural a dirty word for a while. Eventually, there will be monaural records again. If it is newly-recorded, it will be stereo; if it is anciently-recorded it will be monaural because that is the way it is. These distinctions will not exist anymore. Once you let the retailers clear their shelves of low-priced merchandise, it will stop being a problem.

I would like to comment on proposals for a consortium, or some similar plan, to make more records available. I have already expressed a very cynical reaction because I think that the major labels will only consider such a plan if it happens to be proposed at a time when all three companies happen to have just killed their reissue programs. Actually, they work on an unintentional stagger system. Columbia is now dead, and Victor may be dying, but Decca is still going. As long as one of them is doing reissues you will not get that kind of cooperation.

These records are commercial enterprises. The reason a label such as mine is able to exist is not that we are more altruistic, but that we have a lower overhead. We are a little, marginal company that considers sales of 5,000 damn good — frequently, they are a lot less than that. In my guise as a businessman, as opposed to my guise as a dedicated collector and producer, I make a little money and, unlike Columbia, making a little money is good for me. Columbia cannot make any money at a 3,000- or 4,000-copy sales level.

But even though they let these unsuccessful commercial properties lie dormant forever, there is, on the other hand, Duke Ellington, Louis Armstrong, or blues that become popular. The minds that make the decisions at the major labels are not really capable, nor should we expect them to be, of differentiating between one and the other. They are not going to accept the concept that there is material that they will never use and, therefore, it should be released. That is my negative reaction on the likelihood of success for such a project.

ARCHIVAL PRACTICES

Audience and Panel Discussion

Discussion from the audience centered on the question of getting clearance from recording companies for the inclusion of their records in anthologies. One suggestion was for the Institute of Jazz Studies to involve other institutions in a consortium, which would draft a long-term cooperative project for historical anthologies. Record companies might be more willing to cooperate with a large cooperative undertaking, which would enjoy considerable prestige.

The agreement by the record company would take the form of a leasing of material, with a recapture clause giving the company an option to regain full rights after some specified period. In effect, the company would be putting the material on loan.

A university or other institutional archive would certainly have a better chance than an individual to work out arrangements with record companies. The Library of Congress has made important recordings and then leased them to commercial firms for issuance. And some universities have issued records on their own labels, usually in the classical field. There is some interest in a consortium of universities for the purpose of issuing records, but most universities or university presses are reluctant to get into this difficult area.

THE NEGRO NEWSPAPERS AS SOURCE MATERIALS

Walter C. Allen
Jazz Researcher and Discographer

Previous talks at these conferences have dealt with, among other things, the two main problems of discography: when and where was an item recorded and who are the performers? Other speakers have cited the many sources of information that the discographer has at his disposal: information from the recording companies themselves, interviews, data inscribed in the wax and on the labels of the recordings, and information obtainable by listening. Contemporary literature (trade papers, show-biz journals, newspapers, and the like) may also yield useful information to the person diligent enough to wade through this material, and today I am going to show you some of the kinds of information, useful to the jazz historian and discographer, that I have found in the Negro press.

I make no claim to being the first one to search these journals. Bill Russell, Fred Ramsey, Charles Edward Smith, George Hoefer, John Steiner, Frank Driggs, Len Kunstadt, Paul Larson, and undoubtedly many others have done some similar research, and their findings have been incorporated in many books and articles. Few, however, have cited specific sources for specific items of information, and, in a few cases, incorrect dates have even been cited.

All the Negro newspapers of my acquaintance were weeklies, usually appearing on Saturdays, and ranging from four-page sheets of almost primitive appearance to large issues of 30 or more pages using the most up-to-date printing methods. Some were for a strictly local or regional market, others had columns or pages from all over the country and had a national circulation. Their primary purpose was to circulate news of interest to the black people of their market area.

The following list names the papers with which I am acquainted; first are those that are important to the jazz historian of the 1920s and 1930s, in the sense that they produced large amounts of interesting information over long periods.*

Baltimore *Afro American*
Chicago *Defender*
Philadelphia *Tribune*
Pittsburgh *Courier*
New York *Age*
New York *Amsterdam News*

Except for some bound volumes of the *Courier* from 1947-1953 at Rutgers, these are all on microfilm.

Next are those that yield occasional items of interest:
Cleveland *Gazette*
Norfolk *Journal and Guide*
Savannah *Tribune*
Washington *Bee* (1920-1922 only)
California *Eagle* (Los Angeles)

The above list is not exhaustive; newspapers were published for the Negro market in other cities. Indianapolis had its *Freeman* (Princeton's files stop in World War I period), St. Louis had its *Argus*, New Orleans and Detroit had papers, and so on. Kansas City, Houston, Atlanta, Boston, Birmingham, among others, may also have had such media as well. I simply have not run across them at any library conveniently available to me. I have no idea what Negro papers the Library of Congress might have. Perhaps this paper will encourage others to investigate this further.

Let us now consider the types of information which might from time to time be found in these media, and which would interest the jazz researcher. Mostly, it is found on the amusement page(s) usually present in the first group of papers, and sometimes found in the second group. Up to the mid-1920s, the emphasis on these pages was on vaudeville and personal appearances; by the late 1920s, this had given way to movies as the prime entertainment medium. These pages are especially productive of news and advertisements of playing engagements and of new record releases, up through the late 1920s.

For example, the *Afro American* of December 2, 1921, carried a review of the performance at the Regent Theater in Baltimore, of Ethel Waters and her Black Swan Troubadours. In addition to descriptions of her appearance, her wardrobe, and her voice, the review listed the personnel of her accompanying unit:

*All of the newspapers listed, except the Philadelphia *Tribune* and Washington *Bee*, are in the Schomburg Collection of the New York Public Library. The two noted exceptions are in the Princeton University Library.

All, except the New York *Age*, Savannah *Tribune*, and California *Eagle* are also in the Princeton University Library.

The Philadelphia *Tribune* is also available in the Philadelphia Public Library.

The Pittsburgh *Courier*, from 1947 on, is also in the Rutgers University Library.

"Her Jazz Boys are composed of Charles E. Jackson, violin; P. Bushell, clarinet; Augustus Aiken, cornet; Joseph Elder, tenor saxophone; Eugene Aiken, trombone; C. Mosby, bass Saxophone; Raymond Green, drums, and Hamilton Henderson, piano. The latter is also manager of the recording department of the Pace Phonograph Company."

Hamilton Henderson is better known to us as Fletcher Henderson, Hamilton being his middle name; the Pace Phonograph Company manufactured the Black Swan record, and was the first black-owned-and-operated phonograph recording company in this country. This tour of Ethel Waters and her troupe was undertaken to publicize the artists and recordings issued by Black Swan, and was Henderson's first important playing engagement.

Jazz historians tend to emphasize the importance of specific playing engagements in the careers of certain artists. An example is the engagement of King Oliver's Dixie Syncopators at the Plantation Cafe in Chicago, which lasted for two full years (1925-1927) and during which he recorded frequently. The following advertisement from the Chicago *Defender*, May 23, 1925, typical of many, perhaps serves to place in proper perspective the fact that the Oliver band was only one group of performers at the Plantation. If we may believe the priority of listing and the typographical emphases, the potential audience was far more interested in the vaudeville performers than in King Oliver's orchestra.

"PLANTATION CAFE, 35th and Grand Boulevard, The Garden Spot of the South Side, Laurence Deas, Producer of "Shuffle Along" and "Plaintation Days," Presents His

2ND EDITION OF PLANTATION REVUE

Friday, April 10th, Special Music by JOE JORDAN, Featuring ADA BROWN (The Brown Who Sings the Blues); White and Geary, dancers; Phil and Clarice, A Classy Pair; Billy Ledman, Clever Comedian; Lovie Taylor, Dancing Master; Leonidas Simmons, California Song Bird; Al Taylor, Chicago Favorite; And the Greatest Dancing Chorus Ever Seen in a Cabaret, The Plantation Ginger Girls; King Oliver's Dixie Syncopators."

The same page also contains items relating to the appearance of Erskine Tate's Symphony Orchestra at the Vendome Theater (Louis Armstrong later played in this band); Clarence Jones and his Wonder Orchestra at the Owl Theater; Sara Martin at the Palace Theater, Memphis, opening May 25; Clara Smith at the Bijou Theater, Nashville, opening May 25, other acts on the bill including E. S. Coleman, the "Fiddling Sheik," and a "refined bicycle act."

There are a great many advertisements (and usually accompanying news items) heralding the forthcoming appearance of out-of-town dance orchestras at local theaters, dance halls, or amusement parks. The following from the Baltimore *Afro American*, Oct. 19, 1929, is perhaps a typical example:

"The Best of Them All!!! Ain't misbehaving — they're saving it all for you!
FLETCHER HENDERSON and his World Famous Recording Broadcasting Orchestra, just back from the coast. (Photo of Band)
HEAR HIM NOW! At New Albert — Tues. Nite, Oct. 22
Positively as advertised or your money back! They're worth waiting for!
50¢ Before 9 — IKE DIXON, promoter — 60¢ After 9"

Frequent advertisements by the recording companies of the day — Black Swan, Paramount, OKeh, Columbia, Victor — also appeared. They are valuable since they provide, in some instances, the only available estimate of release dates of particular recordings. From the pattern of release dates and matrix numbers the recording date can often be approximated. Occasionally, bits of discographical information appear in the advertisements; for example, the Paramount advertisement in the *Defender* for Feb. 16, 1924, lists Paramount 12064 as one of the new releases, "*Lawdy Lawdy Blues* and *Moanin' Groanin' Blues* sung by Ida Cox Acc. by Blues Serenaders with Tommy Ladiner and his Praying Cornet." The presence of Tommy Ladnier on these recordings has long been known, but his name is not on the record labels and this advertisement does provide contemporary confirmation of his presence.

An important feature of the *Defender's* amusement pages, in particular, was the inclusion of numerous reports and letters from correspondents, who sent in news of the appearance of vaudeville artists, blues singers, bands, etc. at engagements all over the country. Later, in 1925, an important step was taken by the *Defender* when Dave Peyton, a local bandleader, undertook the publication of a weekly column entitled THE MUSICAL BUNCH. This differed from other correspondents' reports (some of which appeared quite regularly under specific bylines) in that it dealt exclusively with orchestral musicians rather than with vaudeville or minstrel performers. It yields a great deal of information about the activities of the black musicians in Chicago during the latter half of the twenties.

For example, one of his early columns in the Chicago *Defender*, Oct. 10, 1925, carries brief sentences or paragraphs telling of the activities of J. W. Wright, a drummer; Joe Oliver's Jazz Band playing a gig at Harmon's Dreamland; Capt. F. E. Dryer, former bandmaster at Tuskegee; William Dawson, trombonist; Gilbert Anderson, a symphonic conductor; Tom Lemonier, songwriter; Mrs. Alice Calloway Walker, drummer and leader of the band at the Indiana Theater (with personnel); the Carroll Dickerson and Sammy Stewart orchestras; Joe Jordan's Sharps and Flats, with a burlesque show; Fletcher Henderson's orchestra, at Roseland, in New York; Darnell Howard, leaving soon to join Jack Carter in the Orient; Tommy Ladnier, writing from Sweden; the forthcoming Local 208 election; Jimmy Wade's and Joe Oliver's bands playing a benefit for soldiers' relatives; Will Vodry's band, playing Chicago with the Florence Mills show; Dave Peyton's band (with personnel) playing a student dance at Champaign, Ill.; and Will Carroll, a violinist, recently moved to Chicago.

Later, many of Peyton's columns were largely devoted to pontifical sermons to the musicians of Chicago exhorting them to come to work on time, to dress neatly, to learn their instruments, to learn music theory, to avoid clown music and low-down blues, and to observe the success of the better white orchestras such as Paul Whiteman and Paul Ash. Occasionally he would cite the "better" Negro orchestras, such as Leroy Smith, Charles Cooke, Sammy Stewart, and Fletcher Henderson.

By the early 1930s, Peyton gave up the column, to be succeeded (with various column titles) in turn by Jerome Carrington, Walter Barnes, and Jack Ellis, all musicians. By 1940, however, this feature was no longer carried by the *Defender*. The New York papers have, at various times, carried columns by "Deacon" Jones, Percy Outram, Dan Burley, Roi Ottley and Ted Yates which contain occasional references to band personnels and engagements. Floyd Snelson had a series of columns and biographies in the *Courier* in the early 1930's.

Besides advertisements and columns, one should look for interviews with currently newsworthy performers, as a source of important biographical information. An example is one in the Baltimore *Afro American* July 27, 1929, bylined by jubilee singer Eva Jessye, interviewing Victoria Spivey, who is here with us today. Victoria was then newly famous for her actress role in the pioneer Negro talkie *Hallelujah.*

On September 29, 1928, a news item in the same paper headlined "Q.R.S. to Enter Race Record Field" tells of the new activities of the QRS piano roll company in preparing to place a line of phonograph records on the market. This was the 7000 series, well-known to collectors. A reference such as this is important in setting a lower floor on the range of possible recording dates for this label.

The earliest known complete account of a Negro recording session is found in the *Afro American,* May 6, 1921:

> "GERTRUDE SAUNDERS MAKES OKEY RECORDS."
> "Gertude Saunders, the clever comedienne of the big 'Shuffle Along' show spent a few days in New York the week of the 18th of April producing two song records for the Okey people.
> "'Daddy' and 'Kiss Me' the two big numbers sung by her in the show and written by Sissle and Blake, who wrote the music and are starring with Miller and Lyles in the attraction, were sung to an accompaniment played by Lieut. Tim Brymm and his Black Devils.
> "The arrangement by Mr. Blake was executed by the following artists personally conducted by Mr. Brymm: Joseph Lymus, violin; W. H. Hicks, first cornet; Albert Foster, second cornet; G. Paris, bass; James Reeny, trombone; Santiago Sanchez, cello; Maylon Hall, clarinet; Geo. Peeks, drums and Isador Unger, organ."

Apart from some spelling errors (should be OKEH instead of Okey; Brymn, not Brymm; Lymas, not Lymus; Revey, not Reeny), this provided a complete personnel for OKeh 8004 by Gertrude Saunders. The first edition of *Blues and Gospel Records* lists this recording as "I'm Craving For That Kind of Love" and "Daddy, Won't You Please Come Home"; dates it as May 1921;

and lists the instrumentation as probably two cornets, trombone, three reeds, violin, banjo, tuba, drums, directed by Tim Brymn, piano. The first title contains the lyrics "Kiss Me, Kiss Me, Kiss Me," so it definitely corresponds to that named in the newspaper. There are some other news items with discographical interest which might be quoted as well.

The examples given so far are typical of what might be found on the amusement pages of these papers. Occasionally, however, items appear on other pages which might be overlooked. For example, the death of a famous entertainment personality, such as Florence Mills or Bessie Smith, might be found on the front page. These are important references to locate, since they unfortunately signify the irrevocable end to a performing and recording career.

A figure of great interest to the record collector is Jimmy Blythe, who played piano on many recordings made in Chicago during the '20s. His name appears only once in the *Defender* in all that time, however, so only the sketchiest picture of his career could even be guessed at. Finally, in the Chicago *Defender*, June 27, 1931, another reference did appear, but to herald his recent death:

> "James Blythe, composer and musician, 30 years old, who lived at 4503 Michigan Avenue, died Sunday. He was a native of Lexington, Ky., and had lived here for 15 years.
> "Blythe had become known throughout the country as the composer of the famous "Mecca Flat Blues," "Chicago Stomp," and "Block and Tackle Blues" as well as several other numbers.
> "The deceased pianist had made records and piano rolls for the Brunswick Recording company.
> "He had studied under Clarence Jones and had achieved fame as an imitator of the Jones style of playing.
> "Besides his widow, Mrs. Janice Blythe, he is survived by three sisters, Mrs. Effie Merritt, Mrs. Mary Slaughter and Mrs. Bessie Clark."

This important obituary provides us for the first time with his birthplace, approximate year of birth (1901), and date of death (probably June 14 or 21, 1931). The reference to him as an "imitator of the (Clarence) Jones style of (piano) playing" comes as a distinct surprise; to the collector, he is regarded as a player of the barrel-house school, from his recordings with Johnny Dodds groups. Clarence Jones, who did make a very few recordings, has never been singled out as a player in that style. Jones led typical movie theater orchestras for many years. Two interpretations may be made:

1) that Blythe's "barrel-house" recordings are in a different style than Jones', which I would conceive of as being rather "straight;"
2) that Jones could in fact play in a real "barrel-house" style which Blythe picked up, but that Jones himself was never recorded playing in that way. If this is the case, we should perhaps reevaluate our conception of Clarence Jones' importance on the Chicago scene.

The death of King Oliver was reported at length on the front page of the

Savannah *Tribune*, April 14, 1938, under the headline "DADDY" JAZZ MUSIC PASSES. This reference gives his birthdate, a brief biography including the fact that Louis Armstrong was his protege, and the circumstances of his last years and death in Savannah. Other reports of his death and his burial were reported in the bigger metropolitan papers, but none of the other obituaries are as sympathetic as this one.

An entirely unexpected discovery was the fact that the local hotels often published guest lists for the past week. Occasionally, the personnel of an orchestra or travelling troupe would be precisely revealed in this manner, as for Pittsburgh's Bailey Hotel in the Pittsburgh *Courier*, August 18, 1934:

> "Fletcher and Horace Henderson, Elme James, Key Johnson, Walter Johnson, William Bailey, Richard Townsend, Ben Webster, Lawrence Lacey, Claude Jones, Russel Smith, Mr. and Mrs. Irving Randolph, all of Fletcher Henderson Orchestra, New York; . . . .
> ". . . . .Eugene Johnson, Claude Hopkins, Fred Norman, Walter Jones, Edw. Jacobs, Bobbie Sands, Albert Snaver, Edmond Hall, Henry Tumel, Fernando Arelo, Claude Hopkins Orchestra, New York."

This particular notice is unique in my experience because it lists the personnels for two orchestras. For the Henderson researcher, it establishes the presence of the band in Pittsburgh in mid-August 1934, and remains the only documentation for what must have been some kind of engagement at that time. There are absolutely no references or advertisements for any Henderson engagement in the *Courier* during that month. Note that the names of Henry Allen, Russell Procope and Hilton Jefferson, then presumably members of the band, are absent; either they stayed in New York this time, or else they registered at some other hotel. The identity of "Richard Townsend" is unknown; if he were a replacement trumpeter or saxist for one of the three missing men, he is not listed in the 802 Directory of that period. Perhaps he was a representative of the booking agency. I have also found personnels for the Bennie Moten band and for McKinney's Cotton Pickers in such hotel register listings. There may well be others which remain to be discovered.

Perhaps my favorite newspaper reference is one which I found quite by accident. It does not occur on the amusement page; but on going slowly through the February 16, 1924, issue of the *Defender*, a familiar photo caught my eye on the society page!

> "MISS LILLIAN HARDIN IS BRIDE OF LOUIS ARMSTRONG"

There were photos of Lil and Louis; a description of the bride's dress; the list of guests, including Fred (Tubby) Hall, Warren Dodds, John Dodds, Bill Johnson, Joseph Oliver, Tom Ladinier, and Raymond Whitsett. Oscar Young's seven-piece orchestra provided music at the reception, and the happy couple were described as members of King Oliver's Creole Band, soon to leave on tour. This stands as the earliest known reference to Louis Armstrong in print, except for his name on record labels as a composer. It predates by 21 months the earliest reference found 30 years ago by William Russell!

This has been a brief summary of the kinds of things that one can find in these old microfilms. There is much more that one would like to find, of course, which is simply not there. The personnels of some bands are NEVER given, some known engagements are not reported, and many that are advertised as "coming" or future events are never mentioned again, so that we do not *really* know whether they, in fact, took place! When there is reportage after the event, practically every engagement was a "big hit", even though it might really have been somewhat less than a success.

For example, when King Oliver took his Dixie Syncopators to New York for two weeks at the Savoy Ballroom in May, 1927, he was reported in the *Defender* as "taking New York by storm." If he was really such a big hit, why could he never get a return engagement there? Very rarely, the reporter was honest and admitted that a certain date was poorly attended or even a flop! In evaluating the information, one needs to use a large dose of common sense and judgement, needless to say.

And of course there is the occasional outright blooper to be found. One in particular comes to mind: a news item of about 1933, in which the English Parlophone issue of Louis Armstrong's 1929 recording "Knocking A Jug" was announced. The item went on to say that Mr. Armstrong had just recorded this song, and that he was assisted by that popular British dance maestro, Jack Teagarden!

There are of course other references which yield information of equal importance: *Billboard, Variety,* the New York *Clipper, Orchestra World,* to name a few. I even found a photo of the Jenkins Orphanage Band of Charleston, S. C., in a most unlikely place — the *National Geographic,* March 1939.

There remains the question, what is to be done with this information that we researchers gather in this way. For my part, I am slowly getting each reference onto a 3 x 5 index card, filed by subject: name of orchestra for which personnel and/or playing engagement date is given; individual names of artists, where they are the subject of a news item or interview or obituary; names and addresses of places where jazz was played; etc. In each case, the newspaper or journal source is detailed so that it can always be relocated. I will be glad to make this data available to any bona fide researcher on a reciprocal basis, and I would like to encourage others, especially in other large cities whose libraries are not convenient for me, to start going through their local papers (white as well as Negro) for similar advertisements and news items. Let's start a central file of these references on a cooperative basis; perhaps the Institute of Jazz Studies could assume a role in this project.

July 27, 1969

SECTION III

Conference on the Preservation and Extension of the Jazz Heritage

INTRODUCTION

William M. Weinberg
Assistant to the President, Rutgers University
Chairman, Advisory Committee for Rutgers Institute of Jazz Studies

This Conference on the Preservation and Extension of the Jazz Heritage is really a continuation of several earlier sessions held by the Rutgers Institute of Jazz Studies. In June of 1968 and this past June, Walter Allen, the Institute's discographer, arranged conferences directed, primarily, at scholars. One outgrowth of those conferences was the identification of two related problem areas.

First, there is a need for people working to preserve the jazz heritage to meet, exchange ideas, and develop more effective programs of preservation. Second, there is the need to use archive materials more effectively.

As a state university and land grant college, Rutgers is concerned with public matters. The University has been providing services to farmers since the Civil War period when the Land Grant Act was passed. More recently it has become increasingly involved in urban problems. With the help of a generous grant from the Ford Foundation some years ago, the Urban Studies Center was established. It has influenced other parts of the University to exchange the isolation of academic life for a more active role in the community. Most recently, Livingston College, a coeducational institution, has been opened. In part, it is the University's response to urban problems and is one aspect of the University's involvement with the community, the state, and the nation.

The Institute of Jazz Studies is a response to the community's aesthetic needs. The archives of the Institute are now out of storage and in the John Cotton Dana library in the Rutgers Library in Newark. It is anticipated that this year the archives may be used to back up academic programs in the area of black studies.

Therefore, this conference will focus on preserving the jazz heritage and putting it to the most effective use in the community.

Richard B. Allen, curator of the Archive of New Orleans Jazz, Tulane University, will deliver the major paper on *The Function of a Jazz Archive.* Dick Allen has been working with the archives in New Orleans for a decade and has probably done more than any other individual on the university level to develop jazz archives.

A panel discussion based on the two focal points of the conference will follow the paper.

THE FUNCTION OF A JAZZ ARCHIVE

Richard B. Allen

Curator, Archive of New Orleans Jazz
Tulane University Library

This paper is about the function, needs, and administration of jazz archives. The future of jazz studies and archives will also be considered. Finally, some of the difficulties of staffing and financing jazz archives will be noted. Throughout the paper, the Archive of New Orleans Jazz of Tulane University will be used as an illustration.

In the simplest terms, the function of a jazz archive is to preserve the jazz heritage, or that portion of the heritage to which a given archive is devoted, and make it available to people who need it or are interested in it. In this context, all of the following discussion is really about how this is being done, how it might be done more effectively, what unique problems arise when working with jazz archival materials, and what solutions might be devised to solve them.

The Archive of New Orleans Jazz was established at Tulane University in 1958. During the previous year I had talked to Dr. William R. Hogan, then Chairman of the History Department at Tulane, about basing a master's thesis on tape-recorded interviews with jazz musicians. It happened that Dr. Hogan himself collected jazz records and was impressed when I told him that I worked for and with Bill Russell, who has made a unique contribution to New Orleans jazz.

Dr. Hogan conceived the Jazz Archive and wrote a proposal which was approved by the Ford Foundation. The foundation gave a grant of $75,000 to establish the Archive, with Russell and myself as principal researchers and Hogan as the administrator. Supplementary grants later brought the total to $150,000.

This money carried the Archive through its initial collecting and cataloging phase, after which the University was committed to operate the Archive as a research center. On July 1, 1965, the Director of the Tulane University Library became responsible for the Archive. Since then we have continued to collect successfully, but to catalog with less success. However, the opening of the Archive has made great demands on our time.

We have over 8,000 records listed and well over 10,000 waiting to be processed; 11,821 sheet music items, about two-thirds of which are band orchestrations; 1,270 reels of tape-recorded interviews; 678 reels of music; 32 reels of film; 5,448 photographs; and over 17,000 other archival items, including books, magazines, newspapers, catalogs, scrapbooks, posters, and notes. In all there are more than 40,000 items. (Totals updated to 1971)

Developing an effective card catalog for jazz presents unusual problems. At present we use an ordinary library card catalog, but have developed our own system of cataloging records, since there is apparently no standard form suitable for a sound recording archive. The Library of Congress phonograph record catalog cards are not very useful because there are too few headings to be added. For instance, the Blue Bechet LP on Victor has as a main entry simply: *Blue Bechet.* Who would ever look this record up under *Blue?* The suggested headings under which it is also filed are *Jazz ensembles* and *Bechet, Sidney.* The headings are typed on the tops of the cards, and the cards are filed alphabetically under "J" for Jazz ensembles and under "B" for Bechet. This might work in an ordinary music library, but a researcher needs more.

In the Archive of New Orleans Jazz, we shelve the records by the label and the catalog numbers. These serve as call numbers. They also serve as a point of entry to identify the record, and, as such, are familiar to collectors and discographers. The headings on the catalog cards, based on the label and any notes accompanying the record are: *leader, sidemen, band name, titles, composers,* and *arrangers.* We omitted matrix and take numbers, a serious error, as any discographer knows. This makes it difficult to find out which take we have without checking the record.

The ideal would be a union catalog and a union discography with maximum data available, and appropriate application of information storage and retrieval methods. The jazz recording union catalog could add many more points of entry including matrix and take numbers, place and date recorded, condition, and any collection possessing records, etc. Although books and magazines are useful in identifying examples of a general subject like blues or ragtime, researchers who are more concerned with classification and cataloging might want additional subject headings. Modern computer technology makes such a system feasible and might ultimately serve as a pilot for a union catalog of all sound recordings. This would be an invaluable research tool.

Storing matrix numbers of little interest to most scholars is important to discographers simply because they know whether a series of numbers is relevant or not. Not only do we need to know when the matrix numbers for a jazz recording date began and stopped, but the adjoining dates may be important clues. Sometimes personnel overlap. Don't over-categorize. For instance, the Alabama Rascals' sessions of March 30 and 31, 1932, and the Big Bill and His Jug Busters' sessions of the same dates probably have some men on all sessions. The numerical listings show that the Alabama Rascals' "Beedle Um Bum" and "Biscuit Roller" were made just before and after Big Bill's "Long Tall Mama." Other matrices are adjacent in the listing.

The jazz union catalog would also help in locating requests for records. Existing catalogs and discographies are not complete or standardized. Where do you find a list of all recordings of a particular tune? How do you add new facts to a discography? Even the loose-leaf ones get out of date, assuming that they are completed in the first place. Discography is now so complex that teamwork is necessary. Since one answer to complexity is centralization, perhaps the ultimate solution is one jazz center.

An additional advantage of such a complete catalog is that the research is less likely to be inadvertently repeated.

On the subject of information retrieval, it should be noted that it is no service to have 200,000 records, as does the Archive at Lincoln Center, if your users do not know what you have. There is a great deal of discussion in the library field now, concerning both books and recordings, about developing an efficient catalog — one that is easy to put information into as well as get information out of — without diluting it beyond usefulness.

Once a computerized program is set up it is rather easy and inexpensive to modify it by adding a loop to a computer program and repunching a card. New and/or contradictory data can be easily added. Information on records is never definitive and often needs further investigation. Even record labels can be wrong. For example, according to Lizzie Miles, J. Russel Robinson accompanied her on "Black Man (Be on Yo' Way)," not Spencer Williams as the label reads. Aural evidence is useful, but doubtful when not confirmed.

The proposed union catalog and existing discographies would provide the basis for a union discography. The need for a research center with these points of entry and the sources of data is obvious. It would be of use to discographers, musicologists, performing musicians, cultural historians, and scholars from many other fields. Even the record companies might use this tool to locate copies of their own records to make masters for reissue. Discographers would find that the rapid sorting techniques and complete storage of information would save time and minimize useless duplication and uncorrected scholarship, etc. We desperately need universally accepted, standardized methods.

In addition to the union catalog, a method of exchanging sound archival material is needed. Why not loan tapes from one archive to another as libraries loan books? A researcher can get books sent to the Tulane library from out-of-town libraries. He can write for Xerox copies of rare archival material. Why not a similar system for sound archives? A taped copy of rare discs or tapes could be sent from one institution to another. Duplicate copies of unique tapes and rare discs could be deposited in another institution for use and as a safety measure.

A brief survey of existing jazz archives and libraries points up the need for coordination among them. Greater cooperation would not only result in more effective use of archival material, but of funds, as well.

In addition to the Library of Congress and the Archive of New Orleans Jazz, there are archival collections at Rutgers, the Arkansas Arts Center, North Texas State University, Emory University, Indiana University, the Smithsonian Institution, the New Orleans Jazz Museum, the European Jazz Federation Library Centre in Brussels, the Jazz Institute of Chicago, and other institutions. Of course, there is a great deal in the individual collector's possession too.

The John D. Reid Collection of American Jazz is housed in the Arkansas Arts Center, Little Rock. The collection contains about 4,000 recordings, all 78s in excellent condition, with emphasis on jazz from 1917 to 1940. It also contains other archival material not described in the literature currently available. Some of the recordings are extremely rare. Doubtless there is a large number of unique copies in the collection. It is cataloged and ready for use, but has not been used. It would be worthwhile to make taped copies to be deposited in other archives both as a safety measure and to make the music available.

North Texas has a large collection of Ellington recordings. In 1969 Emory announced that it had received a collection of 2,000 books dealing with jazz, art, and linguistics.

The Indiana University Archives of Traditional Music consists of taped music and a few interviews. The tapes seem countless in number and are mostly folk music from all over the world, but there is some jazz. The Australian Jazz Archive is being organized in Melbourne.

Much blues, gospel and hillbilly material are in the John Edwards Memorial Foundation at the University of California at Los Angeles.

The Smithsonian has little jazz material, but wants to collect more. The European Jazz Federation is especially concerned with bibliography. There can be no doubt about the need to develop programs and techniques for pooling and exchanging these materials.

The numerous, unique, legal problems involved in reproduction of sound, especially music, further complicate the maintenance of jazz archives. The ownership of recorded music and interviews is not determined. Is it the record company? The composers? The performers? The publisher? All of these, and others? What are the rights of an interviewer? An interviewee? Is a battery of lawyers and a lobby needed in Washington to work on the copyright law? Perhaps the copyright lawyer of the Council on Library Resources should address himself to "this barrel of snakes" as Fred Cole, president of the Council, calls it. Perhaps a test case would clarify some of the legal issues.

An additional limitation on the development of a comprehensive archive is union restrictions. The Archive of New Orleans Jazz, for instance, is allowed to make documentary recordings, but not to copy them. Shouldn't safety copies be deposited in a similar institution? Could one get permission from the union? Can commercially available recordings be copied? Is information on availability available?

The day-to-day use of archive materials presents security problems that must be dealt with. Will researchers sneak copies with small, portable, tape machines? Are the archivists responsible and trustworthy? Are security precautions adequate? Stolen music and interviews might even be sold.

The technical aspects of the standardization of recording and playback equipment, and the storage and preservation of material in sound archives, should be handled by specialists like John Reid, John Steiner, and Robert Carneal of the Library of Congress; M. K. Testerman of the Graduate Institute of Technology, University of Arkansas; and John Colvin of the Audio Engineering Society.

What kind of needle is best for copying 78s in poor condition? What do we do about hill-and-dale records? What is the best base for tapes? How can we cut down on search time for a particular tune on a tape? What about using cartridges? What playback and recording equipment has the lowest maintenance costs? What about print-through? We need to anticipate and try to plan for future developments. The founders of the Archive of New Orleans Jazz never dreamed of stereo when they applied for the Ford grant.

Should all discs be copied on tape? At Tulane the Paramounts and Brunswicks from the depression years have been copied. The rare items in a block can be picked out by catalog numbers. However, all the rarest records have not yet been taped because there has not been time to hunt them down. In addition to being a good safety measure, taping has enabled collectors to give us copies of items not in the Archive.

Interest in the oral history of jazz provided much of the initial impetus in establishing the Archive of New Orleans Jazz, and since 1958 the Archive has acquired over 600 interviews. Alan Lomax is generally credited with the first recorded interview with a jazz musician back in 1938, and one might say that oral jazz history began then. Lomax interviewed Jelly Roll Morton for the Library of Congress, and that interview remains one of the most fascinating and fantastic documents in jazz.

Unfortunately, private individuals did most of the interviews until 1958, and many are not now available. Again, centralization may be the key to systematizing efforts to retrieve these interviews.

Undoubtedly, the oral history aspect of jazz archives will grow in importance. The *American Archivist* carries many articles on oral history. The *Wilson Library Bulletin* of March, 1966, published an oral history symposium, and an Oral History Association has been organized.

Unfortunately, there are no documents on the early development of jazz music. The earliest jazz record known dates back only to 1917, long after the new style began to emerge. Not only were the record companies slow to become interested, but the music was considered too vulgar for anyone to write about. Like so many other aspects of American culture, it was deemed unworthy of any but the smallest notice. Therefore, the memories of musicians, dancers, and others who had an interest in the subject are the primary source on the early days of jazz.

In addition to providing information about the music and their lives, these people create vivid pictures of an era seen from a unique standpoint. The interviews will be of interest not only to jazz scholars and musicians, but also to journalists, anthropologists, sociologists, cultural historians, linguists, musicologists, and folklorists.

The Archive has been developing new interviewing techniques in the post-Lomax period. One new direction involves interviewing obscure musicians and non-musicians, who often give us a new perspective. These supplement interviews with more famous personalities whose answers sometimes seem too pat.

Our interviewers attempt to obtain as relaxed an atmosphere as possible. To make the interviewees less conscious of the tape recorder, the interviews are generally conducted in the interviewees' homes, and are not rigidly structured. A list of suggestions and standard questions is used as a guide, but often the most revealing statements emerge from casual asides and comments. Although biographical data are well documented, the interviewers also encourage the unexpected. Interviewees might ramble from one subject to another and reveal a new facet of their personalities, or suggest a new insight into their music. Some questions are purposely vague to allow latitude in the answers. Explanations are sought rather than simple yes or no responses. If this technique is not productive, then specific questions are asked.*

Fortunately, the interviewees are generally articulate, cooperative, and enjoy reminiscing. Although their formal training is usually limited, they appreciate the value of history and are keenly aware of the development of and changes in musical styles.

Because of the time element, the Archive interviewed the oldest people first. One woman was over 100 years old and sang variants of several hymns. Sick musicians have been interviewed and particularly appreciate the chance to make history and get paid besides. Many of the musicians interviewed have died.

The age of the subjects and the informality of the interviewing technique frequently require putting reminiscences into an historical context to elicit specific information. If the interviewer has a working knowledge of history,

*Much of the above material has been published in the WILSON LIBRARY BULLETIN, March 1966, Vol. 40, No. 7.

especially local history, or can link events to births, deaths, marriages, etc., the interview is often more productive.

Another source of oral history is jazz courses. When guest musicians are invited to discuss and demonstrate jazz styles, their colorful comments, singing, and playing are well worth preserving on tape.

In addition to tapes made by staff members, taped interviews are donated by people interested in jazz. Not all of these are Orleanians; musicians in other localities have been interviewed to provide contrast and to show the diffusion of jazz. Younger musicians from the United States, England, France, Germany, Sweden, and Australia have also been interviewed to document the spread of the idiom.

Tapes are never erased since no written transcription or digest is perfectly accurate. The spoken work expresses feelings which cannot be duplicated on paper. Also, it is easy to misunderstand the recorded word. For example, one secretary, in transcribing a tape, wrote "liar" for "lawyer," a grave error. Another wrote "Maple Leaf Rag" as "Make Believe Rag."

A further complication is that colloquial usage, local idioms, and trade jargon can be confusing: "musician" means one who reads music as opposed to a "head" or non-reading player. A jazzman who relies solely on his ability to improvise is simply not a musician in some circles. Therefore, the tapes are retained as reliable primary source material.

Originally, it was thought necessary to write down every word the musicians said. Later it was decided that, in the interest of time, a brief digest with editorial comments would satisfy most research needs and would make the material more readily available.

Paul Crawford, a professional trombonist, arranger, and graduate of the Eastman School of Music, did most of the summaries of the interviews. His wide acquaintance and playing experience with musicians are a valuable background for writing up their interviews. After he completed a draft, it was checked against the tape and, if necessary, editorial comments are added. The tapes are then indexed with references to people as well as bands, places, and other subjects.

So that the taped material may be used by researchers, the interviewees sign releases which permit quoting of their exact words. If they refuse to sign, the interview may be cited, but not quoted.

Unfortunately, there has been too little use of the interviews. Researchers are much more interested in phonograph records. They are enjoyable and an ideal starting point if you cannot get live music, and are good historical documents as well. The Archive not only has New Orleans jazz on disc, but also examples of the folk, popular, and classical music which provided the background of New Orleans music. In addition, there are some records of later developments in jazz.

Although enormous progress has been made in recording and preserving jazz, there are still areas which deserve more attention. Barry Martyn, an English drummer and owner of a documentary record company, suggests finding more unissued sound recordings and making more documentary recordings of existing music, especially functional music. Almost-lost styles can be recreated through imaginative planning of band personnel and the use of old scores.

More air shots should be issued. These are often excellent demonstrations of how a band played on a dance job as contrasted to its studio work.

The use of film as a documenting technique could be expanded. Films should be made documenting the music and musicians. Folk instrumental techniques which will otherwise be lost might be preserved on film. In another area, instrumental instructional films using animation and slow motion can demonstrate things a music teacher never could.

Finally, written notes by observers and participants are invaluable as a documentary source because newspapermen and jazz writers have generally neglected current happenings. New Orleans journalists ignore many of the jazz traditions which are kept alive as part of community life. For example, the neighborhood dance halls continue to hire jazzmen; the Masons employ jazz brass bands in laying the cornerstone of a church; and Orleanians still put jazz to its original use as dance music for private parties. These events seldom make the newspapers in New Orleans. Charlie Suhor in *Downbeat* of June 12, 1969, discusses jazz and the New Orleans press at great length. The situation is not confined to New Orleans since jazz exists underground all over the country and throughout much of the world.

Another need is adequate space for efficient working conditions, something too often ignored in colleges and universities. In addition to enhancing the operation of an archive, space enables it to accept donations from private collectors, estates, etc.

I believe that the need for a ragtime archive, a blues and spiritual archive, and even a rock and roll archive is apparent. The latter illustrates how quickly material becomes scarce. Try to find a rock magazine from 1952.

Who has used the Archive of New Orleans Jazz? Among them are jazz musicians, generally foreign, also some record collectors and discographers. Others are people who are just curious, visitors from abroad sent to us by the State Department, mass media people, especially writers, TV producers, and film makers. There have even been a few students and teachers, but the fact that so few have used the Archive is a disappointment to me.

These, then, are some of the things necessary for a jazz archive to preserve effectively and make available the jazz heritage: a union catalog and complete discography specifically designed and indexed to meet the requirements peculiar to jazz studies, a standardized system for the exchange and distribution of archival materials, clarification of union regulations and legal technicalities governing jazz materials, standardization of recording and playback equipment, more written coverage of jazz activities, and space and equipment for efficient operations and expansion.

How these needs, and others, are to be met brings us to the question of staffing and financing. Recruiting staff members is a major consideration in any organization. There are no standards of scholarship or established requirements for a jazz archivist or administrator.

It is possible that a type of interdisciplinary approach would be useful. For example, discographers are qualified to examine and identify recordings, and musicians are knowledgeable about sheet music, while historians, sociologists, and anthropologists can contribute by placing jazz in its historical, social and cultural context. In addition, the research discipline and techniques of social scientists are useful tools in jazz research.

Perhaps some sort of clearinghouse of personnel references or a screening committee would simplify hiring procedures.

As a corollary, young people with ears, some brains, and an interest in jazz must be encouraged and ultimately trained as jazz archivists. Notice the kids who come to hear jazz, who play jazz, who collect records, who do research. They have experience and insights that no school can provide. Competent, interested people should be encouraged to explore jazz studies as a possible profession. Volunteers can do good work, but their duties should be carefully explained and supervised.

The staff needs flexibility to produce. The most important work is out of the shop. You can find valuable 78s and photographs in junkshops, provided you can get out from behind the desk. You have to meet people who can help you, especially collectors and musicians.

Paul Crawford, who works in the Jazz Archive once played trombone with Al Ballanco's band. Ballanco mentioned that he had parts of John Robichaux's library of stock arrangements. Naturally, the Archive obtained them, and they are the one collection that interests young musicians most. In fact, there are three LP's made from these arrangements. Personal contacts are invaluable.

Money from educational and philanthropic institutions does not come to jazz projects in any amount approaching the real needs of researchers and students. There is often a reluctance to accept any new musical style and it is reflected in the difficulty of changing curriculum and facilities to meet new needs and interests.

Moreover, most universities are over-committed, and state universities may be subject to the pressures and interests of politicians. For various reasons, some of which are economic, there is little community support for art centers. All this signifies a lack of support for jazz and jazz studies that results in compromises and policies which, though necessary perhaps for the survival of an archive, curtail its effectiveness.

The Archive of New Orleans Jazz is without funds to fulfill properly and maintain the intent of its grants. The budget did not allow for the purchase of a complete sound system. It was decided that the best equipment, within reason, should be obtained even though this meant having only one turntable and one amplifier for two listening booths. Eventually more electronic equipment will be bought. Since cheap playback equipment means unsound equipment and false economy, it is believed that the present equipment will save on maintenance costs.

Paradoxically, the success of the Archive has become one of its problems. Originally the Archive was conceived of as primarily an oral history project. However, donations of records and sheet music from collectors and record companies and heavy usage of the Archive have created a substantial backlog in cataloging, shelving, tape transcriptions, and filing.

The only solution is foundation grants and gifts of large sums of money from rich alumni and jazz lovers. The alumni look richer than the jazz lovers. Getting grants requires time, again a precious item. You must have also a good imagination, the ability to write, a talent for selling and organizing, and a lucky break. Somehow, contact someone in power who likes jazz and appreciates its importance; its meaning. He can find the right foundation and ram a project through.

An urgent matter is supporting individual researchers before it is too late to get at the data. They are first-rate scholars. Why shouldn't a jazz discographer or an oral historian get some help? Foundations give grants to fiction writers — why not to individual jazz researchers? They do invaluable work.

These are some of my ideas on jazz research and research tools. Perhaps your job will be easier with my suggestions for the developing of a union catalog and discography, the exchanging of tapes of music and interviews, and increased use of film and written notes. I hope to see improved archives, better cooperation among archives, and more effective use of archival materials.

COLLECTION AND PRESERVATION OF JAZZ MATERIALS

David Hall
Head, Rodgers and Hammerstein Archives of Recorded Sound
Lincoln Center, New York

Two pervasive, overriding problems that affect both commercial and noncommercial sound recordings are, first, coordination and dissemination of information concerning what exists and where it is available for audition or copying, and, second, provision for permanent preservation and maximum audition availability at least for unique documentary sound recordings.

Compared to the magnitude of the task, organizational and technological facilities and financial commitments remain in a primitive stage. The goal should be a computerized union catalog with maximum access. Similarly, retrieval of recorded sound should be possible through a cable or satellite network.

Such a network would, of course, be devised with provision for the safeguard of copyrights or proprietary rights. Because this is a gray area, legally, institutional policies at present vary in dealing with the problem. However, individuals and organizations, among them the Association for Recorded Sound Collections, as well as archives, are exploring the development of ground rules to facilitate circulation of unique or commercially unavailable recordings, even in the absence of a revised copyright law.

Presently, worldwide holdings of sound recordings are divided among commercial record companies, broadcasters, educational institutions, specialty shops catering to collectors, and private collectors. Attempts have been made, with varying degrees of success, to gather information on these holdings and their availability through catalogs, copies of dealer listings, discographies, and directories.

A number of European countries have made major headway in developing their own national sound archives. Archival work in the United States, however, has progressed at an uneven pace. Though the Library of Congress in Washington, D.C., has the greatest quantity of archival sound recordings, the Rodgers and Hammerstein Archives of Recorded Sound at the New York Public Library remains, as of 1969, the only general archive offering a full range of audition and reference services.

With the hoped for expansion of the Library of Congress facilities, plus the development of major archives at Stanford University in California, the Boston Public Library, and elsewhere, on-premise audition and research facilities in major metropolitan and university centers can be expected to grow significantly during the 1970s. In addition, the existence of specialized, university-based archives covering jazz, Latin-American music, ethnic music, and oral history should be noted.

All of these facilities could eventually develop into basic coordinating and organizing centers. I think that information retrieval and storage should be coordinated, while the actual work of research and collating in specific areas should be decentralized. All these facilities could eventually serve as basic coordinating and organizing units to feed a centralized cable satellite service envisioned for the future. Meanwhile, the problem of improving the preservation and audition accessibility for out-of-print commercial recordings and for non-commercial materials remains an immediately pressing one.

The problem of preservation alone is enormous. Rodgers and Hammerstein Archives is trying to get 16-inch acetates into what I call first stage preservation onto tape. This is merely the first stage, because tape is not a permanent preservation medium. We would hope eventually to go one step further, particularly since we are working with acetate originals, and get the tape back onto a vinyl disc.

Cassettes are a promising innovation, not necessarily for preservation, but for on-premise listening. Individual cassettes could be used in carrells without running the risks of damage to the original tapes or discs.

Many phases of the preservation job should, ideally, be cooperative university-library endeavors.

It is of interest to note that a certain number of American record labels, specializing in the field of twentieth century music, including jazz, are connected directly or indirectly with universities or university presses. Expanding the roles of universities and university presses in this area, especially in collaboration with commercial firms, to make available out-of-print recordings of unique documentary value would help in the work of preservation and audition accessibility services.

Finally, on the subject of information retrieval (I deal with it every day at Lincoln Center), it does not help anyone to have 200,000 records in stacks if users do not know what you have. There is a great deal of discussion in the library field now in connection with both books and sound recordings, about how to develop the most usable form of catalog allowing for the quickest retrieval of information. The problem is to do it economically and with minimal dilution of the information.

INFORMATION RETRIEVAL

Gerald Jahoda
Professor, School of Library Science
Florida State University

I would like to open my remarks with a personal note. About two years ago I visited New Orleans with my wife, who was working on a biography of the English composer Frederick Delius. She was looking for evidence that would connect Delius's music with the music of the American Negro. Dick Allen took us to see the great, and now late, New Orleans bass player, Slow Drag Pavageau. Slow Drag was able to tell her that one of Delius's melodies was that of an African dance performed at Congo Square at the turn of the century. This turned out to be very valuable information. The point is that the best way to learn about events from the past is to ask people who were there.

This, of course, is not always possible and researchers are forced to rely on the records of the past. In jazz there are the archives containing performances of the musicians and their recorded thoughts on music and life in general. These archives are a treasure of American music, culture, and history which may well be buried and remain undiscovered unless researchers can get to the individual nuggets contained therein.

We cannot say the researchers now have access to these nuggets. This makes their task more difficult and time-consuming than necessary and may even divert their attention to other fields — fields for which records are better organized. But things need not be this way. We now have tools to provide researchers access to the records of jazz (records defined here in the broad sense of the word as phonodiscs, tapes, films, posters, letters, and other documents), if we are willing to make a relatively small investment in time and money.

The researcher in jazz is faced with needs for access to the records similar to those of a researcher in any other field. Similarly, information storage and retrieval techniques now used in science and technology, particularly techniques that utilize computers, can be employed to assist the researcher in jazz.

An information storage and retrieval system should do at least two things for a jazz researcher:

(1) It should enable him to identify records having certain characteristics in common. In the case of phonodiscs these characteristics may be the musician, the instrument, the tune, the date of the recording, and the style of the music. The researcher should be able to query the system for records that have either a single characteristic or any combination of characteristics in common.

(2) The system should also enable the researcher physically to locate copies of the records identified in the search, no matter in which archive they happen to be.

Time does not permit a detailed description of the procedure needed to accomplish these things, but a simplified description is useful. Let us assume that we have examined each record in our archives and that we have identified its characteristics by tagging it according to name of musician, instrument, selection, date and place of recording, and any other identifying characteristics. We will call these characteristics the access points in our system since we will be able to obtain the records indexed in the system by individual characteristics or any combination of these characteristics.

The task of identifying the characteristics of each record may already have been done for us either entirely or in part, in the case of phonodiscs included in discographies. We will also give each record a unique tag for identification, as is done for selections on phonodiscs listed in discographies. The physical location, both in a given archive and within the archive, is also noted for each record. This completes the description of contents and location of the records.

The information for all of the records in all jazz archives or a selected portion thereof, will give us the intellectual "raw material" for our information storage and retrieval system. The raw material is then converted into a form which the computer can process by keypunching on tabulating cards or other means. The information about each record in machinable form is then fed to a computer which can be instructed to do several things.

It can search the index and print out identification codes of records that have desired characteristics in common. It can also search the index periodically for all newly entered records with specified combinations of characteristics of interest to individual researchers. We could then notify researchers of the existence of new records of interest to them. It is also possible to have the computer prepare printed and manually searched indexes that could be deposited in the individual archives and researchers' offices.

The index that makes possible searches for combinations of characteristics is called a coordinate index. Coordinate indexes have been used extensively to organize scientific and technological records. There are computer programs available for searching coordinate indexes, and for the preparation of bibliographies and printed indexes. I believe that computer-aided coordinate indexes to the contents and location of jazz records, the union catalog mentioned in

Richard Allen's paper, could go a long way toward making such records available to researchers.

REFERENCES

Buchanan, J.R. and Hutton, F.C. "Analysis and Automated Handling of Technical Information at the Nuclear Safety Information Center," *American Documentation,* 18: 235—41 (1967).

Lipetz, B.A. "Information Storage and Retrieval." *Scientific American,* 215 (3): 224—42 (Sept. 1966).

Meadow, C.T. *The Analysis of Information Systems. A Programmer's Introduction to Information Retrieval.* New York: John Wiley, 1967.

Starke, A.C. et al. "GAF Document Storage and Retrieval System," *American Documentation,* 19: 173—80 (1968).

NEW VIEWS ON PRESERVATION

Jerry Valburn
Staff Engineer
Mutual Broadcasting System

Before I discuss new views on preservation, permit me to digress, briefly, to a subject which affects all jazz research — copyright law. Having worked in recording studios and networks for many years, I have found that the copyright law, which is extremely vague, is primarily designed to prosecute the individual or the company that actually reproduces and sells material. Laws on copies of acetates or tapes are almost nonexistent.

Years ago at a prominent recording studio in New York a distinguished musician came in for copies of a particular item off the air. Copies were made and the words "reference recording" were stamped on the label of the disc. This meant that the recording studio that did the transfer would not be held responsible, that this was specifically a reference recording to be used as such, and not to be used for commercial purposes.

However, today, with the advent of magnetic recording and tape, the number of tape recorders around is frightening. I shuddered to read about a year ago in one of the trade papers that a new type of recorder was being offered. It was an ad geared to the teenagers, urging them to tape their favorite songs from the radio.

Years ago I remember reading in the *Record Changer*, that the government said it is illegal to take anything off the air and then offer it for sale. In other words, they would not carry such an advertisement then. Yet, with the advent of the LP's, we find that the major record companies — Decca, Columbia, and Victor — are starting to issue recordings in the classical and jazz fields that were taken from broadcasts.

With the law as vague as it is, I believe that between archives there should be no fear that copies can be made. I believe that individuals who are serious students, who do not intend to take material and sell it for profit, should find institutions and archives open to them. They, in turn, should make their own personal jazz libraries available to scholarly institutions. The point is that the thrust of this material and judgement in its use should be determined by the librarians.

Now back to a consideration of the preservation of materials. No one today, many years after the initial use of tape, knows how long tape will last. I have a 20-year-old son, and when he was a very small boy I recorded him at one of the radio stations at which I was working. I'm happy to say that the particular tape, though it is acetate, even today has no print-through. It's a bit on the brittle side though, so I made a copy of it.

With the advent of video tape, the companies such as 3M, that primarily produce and develop tape, were forced to provide a coating that would deliver frequency responses far beyond that of the audio spectrum. They came up with new formulas, coatings, and a tape that gives the audio archivist the widest range of recording at slower speeds, and eliminates such problems as print-through, tape hiss, and brittleness. The advances in the past three or four years in this area have been immense and soon there will be a new breakthrough with the use of chromium as a tape base.

Probably the most important advance in tape is the cassette tape cartridge. Very few people realize what this has done commercially. For years, record companies wanted to market a library of tapes of actual performances that were also available on LP. They realized that a lot of people had tape recorders, a great many more would buy tape and, therefore, they tried to offer at the lowest available price a pre-recorded tape that could be bought in the same store that sells LP's

Many people were reluctant to buy tapes because they were afraid of handling them. Handling can be a problem — getting your fingerprints on an acetate can deteriorate the surface, for instance. It was not until the development of the cassette that tape became a serious market.

In March 1968, CBS began taking all its original 16-inch acetates, famous broadcasts such as Mercury Theatre, music shows, and programs of the '30s and '40s and storing all of them on master cassettes.

In the cassette, as we know it today, the tape moves at a speed of 1-7/8 inches per second and the frequency response is quite good — up to and including 10,000 cycles. Most of our early recordings in both the commercial shellac records, as well as the acetates, do not go much beyond that particular frequency and when these cassettes are played on good equipment, they have a good frequency range. You hear not only the original sound but the harmonics.

This is important because colleges that have started to store tapes from original materials are often reluctant to let a novice walk into their libraries, ask for a particular tape, and put it on the machine himself. If, in winding a tape to get to a specific selection fast forward, something goes wrong and the tape jams, spills, or snags, then the master is damaged or destroyed. With cassettes it is unlikely that such an accident will occur.

I am not suggesting that all materials in our archives be stored only on cassettes. I believe a double system should be set up whereby the best possible tape and the best possible transfer equipment available today are used to make both a reel-to-reel master and a cassette. Then, if another college requests a copy of something, a cassette may be dubbed onto another cassette and sent out. The college, in turn, can either play it back on a cassette system or transfer it to a reel-to-reel tape.

I have actually worked out a system which includes equalizer, pre-amps, speakers, two stereo reel-to-reel professional tape machines, and two cassette machines which would handle every recording and playback function of an archive. This entire system could be set up and operated for under $3,000. The components in a system like this would be of the highest quality, could be as maintenance and trouble free as possible, and, most important, would get the original material onto tape and make it available to those who need it.

All cassettes today come in little plastic boxes and frequently in mailing forms. They weigh only a couple of ounces and are easily mailed. They require no threading; they drop into cassette machines, buttons are pressed, and the material is heard.

I also believe that in the future we will eventually return to records. I know collectors who have kept their cutting equipment and have taken tapes and made acetate safeties of their material. Vinyl is an expensive proposition because it involves pressing material. Unless a way is found to engrave directly onto the vinyl material itself, the three-step master and pressing process would be prohibitively expensive. One must work from a tape to a lacquer, to a metal mother, and, finally, to the record. Of course, when this is done, more than one copy can be produced and made available to institutions, but you would run afoul of the copyright laws.

I suggest that tapes be carefully checked every few years for signs of deterioration. If there are any, then record a tape, keeping the original and a safety.

In my own extensive library I have tapes from 1951-52 and, happily, I have had very little loss or damage. I hope, unless we are hit with a magnetic bomb or sun spots of great magnitude, that they will remain in good condition.

The risks of damage or breakage are too high to permit access to original records. I doubt that many collectors or institutions would allow their original materials to be handled. Tape, then, seems to be the easiest and most effective method for preserving jazz materials and, at the same time, making them available with minimal risks.

REALITIES OF LIBRARY OPERATION

Roy L. Kidman
Former University Librarian
Rutgers University

Many people working in jazz collection and preservation wonder why academic libraries have not been quicker to pick up the possibilities for jazz archives. I will discuss what I think are some of the reasons.

First of all, it has to do with librarians and their attitudes. Librarians, for the most part, work up through the library system very much as teachers do, and a person becomes the head of a library much as one becomes a school principal. A good librarian may not be a good administrator, but he becomes one anyway. I suspect that Peter's law applies: a person progresses through the system until he reaches a position in which he is incompetent and he moves no further.

Librarians usually have backgrounds in the humanitics and social sciences. I do not think I know of a major university librarian who has a music background. They are people who have studied history and English literature and are steeped in the traditions which regard libraries as institutions which handle books.

This is obviously changing and librarians have been forced to accept such technical innovations as microfilm because the original books are unavailable, expensive, or not in usable physical condition. Nevertheless, there is a traditional attitude that bibliography is much more comfortable than discography. A similar situation exists regarding faculty or academic support for jazz. History departments are not primarily interested in jazz history. In a typical English department one is likely to encounter a Renaissance man who thinks it charming and interesting to study jazz, but suggests that it be done on your own time.

Music departments are even more resistant. They are very much like English departments and prefer to let enough time elapse so that they can discover the real fossils — they are not going to identify them early.

Of course, on every campus there is a great deal of interest in jazz among students and some faculty and staff. But even the experience of the Archive of New Orleans at Tulane has been disappointing in that there was little straight academic interest from faculty and students — curiosity, interest in entertainment, moral support — but not the sort which accords it much status in the academic community.

There are academic programs in which interest in jazz has been incorporated into a formal setting. Urban studies, for instance, is concerned with jazz as a cultural phenomenon. However, there is no focus or concentration, specifically, on jazz. Many of the large universities now have 5,000 to 10,000 graduate and professional students in residence at any given time, but it is unlikely that more than four or five of them are doing research or graduate work in jazz.

Ultimately, these attitudes are reflected in the amount of money academic institutions will devote to jazz preservation and study. Jazz requirements go well beyond books. It is true that many of these needs — tapes, recording and playback equipment, etc. — are expensive. However, university library budgets now (many are over $1,000,000 for books and materials alone) could meet that expense.

It is in the areas of space, equipment, and staffing that budgets are most limited. Each budget has guidelines, restrictions, really: you cannot use "people money" for "things," you cannot use "equipment money" for "people," and you cannot recapture salary fragments. There is a myriad of rules which makes it impossible for even fairly sensitive administrators to operate a library so that it takes the greatest advantage of its resources.

The budgeting system has gotten so restrictive that in the University of California they have a formula: we know from past experience that 5 percent of your staffing needs will not be filled because there will be people retiring or leaving, and you don't get a new person right away, so 5 percent of your total budget is not really necessary. So, they give you money for your staff and then take 5 percent away again immediately.

When you begin to work within this kind of framework, you have people deciding that someone from the aircraft industry should help us with the budget and that we should have a kind of cost benefit figure for expenditures. How do you explain what the cost benefit is going to be for a jazz archive to a young computer expert from Lockheed? When you begin to get to the things that really show, such as space, staffing, and so forth, you get into a very tight situation. You know you should be able to do more than it would appear from the size of the budget, but you're not able to.

It seems that I am describing a sort of confluence of apathies, at worst, and I'm afraid that the best is not much better. However, I hope it is not so discouraging that you stop trying to improve the levels of jazz study and preservation.

VISUAL JAZZ

Frederic Ramsey, Jr.
Author, Producer, and Photographer

Sixteen years ago, in the summer of 1953, when the announcement of the formation of the Institute of Jazz Studies appeared in *The Record Changer*, it included a photographic documentary which I had done earlier, and it was introduced in this way: "Although this document was created by Ramsey as an individual, he is quick to point out that it is very much an example of the sort of project that can be developed under the auspices of the Institute of Jazz Studies and illustrates the new dimensions in jazz research the Institute seeks to encourage." That was 16 years ago and I have been concerned about visual preservation of jazz material much longer than that.

There is really no archive that does anything about visual material related to jazz. There are beginnings here and there, but, so far, no systematic effort has been made in that direction. We have informed amateurs like Ernie Smith and John Baker whose work has been outstanding; as far as I know theirs are the most important collections of film.

At this stage, when we are all trying to interest more people in jazz and various kinds of American music, the visual element is particularly significant. This is an audio-visual world — there is the "track," or sound, that goes with film and television, and its essential companion, the "camera," or "visual," requirement. Take either one away and you diminish the effectiveness of your communication system.

We are all aware that there is not enough support for programs that, perhaps, deserve top priority, so it is discouraging to talk about film, the most expensive medium of all. However, although the idea of setting up a film library of historical and contemporary material is still in the dream stage, it is useful to explore the need for such an archive and how it might be developed.

There is an enormous demand for film in almost every area of communication and education. I have an extensive file of requests for visual material from more than 25 different sources: American and foreign publishers and TV networks; university presses; encyclopedias; magazines; authors; scholars; makers of educational films and audio-visual teaching aids; teachers developing courses in jazz, the dance, studies in American civilization, studies in black heritage and music-making — to name only a few. It is not an exhaustive list, but it indicates the scope of the need for a visual resources bank.

The collection would include moving pictures from as far back as 1898, still photographs from 1840, and art and sculpture. Such a bank, or if you will, the Visual Archive of the Institute of Jazz Studies at Rutgers University, would acquire, store, catalog, and make available all the known material that can be *seen* that relates to jazz. All visual material could be assembled at one place, or made available for sharing through a consortium of archives. This would speed and proliferate production of books, film, and television.

No discussion of jazz film preservation can proceed without acknowledging a great debt to Ernie Smith. His list of films in the *Jazz Dance* book written by Marshall and Jean Stearns is more than just a beginning. I doubt if the book could have been so thoroughly researched and convincingly written without the film material that Smith has so painstakingly collected. It is an excellent example of the kind of collaboration that can exist between researchers of visual material and students of jazz. The proposed archive would be devoted to acquiring and making usable and available all the known bits of film that relate to jazz-making, jazz locales, jazz performances, and jazz musicians.

Ernie Smith has proved that there is a great deal available, and it seems inevitable that more will show up. There are, too, contemporary sources from which material can be requested. Many TV and film documentaries have "out-takes" valuable to the jazz researcher, and many films made of music consist of several "takes," alternates of which should be solicited.

Among the tasks of a jazz film archive would be the compilation of a history of jazz on film. At present, no intelligently presented, well-edited, comprehensive history exists. This would be essential to the archive and viewers everywhere.

Another requirement would be the development of a catalog of available materials and, as a corollary, perhaps, a catalog of sources with descriptions of what they include.

New film productions by the archive might include interviews, general documentaries, and demonstrations of musical techniques by living musicians.

The use of still photographs of jazz and jazz-related subjects is now so widespread that no special pleading for its relevance to an archive is required. Still photos are used in almost every area of publishing and are in demand as the basis of large-mount exhibitions, in slide shows, and lecture demonstrations. Recent noteworthy exhibits based on stills are the *Harlem on My Mind* show at the Metropolitan Museum; an exhibit made up by the New Orleans Jazz Museum, which has had exposure abroad; another about blues by USIA, in England; and my own *Where the Music Started* which is touring college campuses. All the TV networks need stills of jazz material and have developed a new technique for using them. The still print, mounted on an easel, can be explored, photographically, by cinematographers who move in and around the subjects, zoom in and out of them, make them dance, etc.

There are many sources of still films, and only a concerted effort could produce the truly comprehensive collection that will be needed by future historians, program producers, and book publishers.

A logical outgrowth of such a collection would be the production by the archive of exhibits and slide shows, synchronized to available sound, or use of stills in educational films.

Jazz-related art, sculpture, and reproductions are territories that have had little exploration. However, from the earliest periods there have been art works which suggest correlations to jazz material—early bas-reliefs, friezes, mosaics, scratchings—which portray early music-making in Africa, the Mediterranean Basin, and the Near and Far East.

During the nineteenth century in this country, artists with sketchbooks roamed and observed, illustrated, and recorded. Some of their works are reproduced in books and magazines of the period, such as *Harper's*, *The Century Magazine*, and many others. Many of their drawings offer fresh insights to early black music-makers, especially in the Deep South.

Sheet music covers and catalogs of music and musical instruments are all potential sources of fresh and exciting graphic materials.

There are as many sources as there are techniques of reproduction — woodblock, chromos, steel engraving, lithography, to name a few. A documentary, graphic history of jazz and pre-jazz music-makers in the United States, exploiting these sources, would be an appropriate project for a film archive. A further projection of this sort of collection would be exhibits based on innovative use of early material.

Clearly, we may not be able to do much about it now, but there can be no question that the visual side of the jazz heritage must rank equally with other archival projects. It is an inevitable part of this heritage, and it belongs.

JAZZ AND AFRO-AMERICAN STUDIES

Alvin Batiste
Jazz Musician and Faculty Member
Southern University

During 1969, an Institute in Jazz will be opened at Southern University in Baton Rouge, Louisiana. The predominantly black universities in the United States have shown this interest in jazz studies only recently. But, as we move together to bring about a more unified experience in American life, I hope that I can contribute, through the Institute at Southern, to the erasing of this condition.

To my mind, jazz and Afro-American studies are inseparable. Indeed, they are inseparable in American and human studies, so although I have not prepared a formal talk, I have assembled some ideas related to the existence of the Institute itself. If the Institute has to have a title, let it be Jazz and Being.

Now Jazz and Being is a real thing. It is human beings involved with the totality of environmental problems combined with aesthetic goals and ideals. An article entitled "Jazz and Being" in the *Rosicrucian Magazine* is appropriate to what I feel, what I've experienced, what I would like to see happen, and what has been heard today.

The article noted that the history of jazz is an example of the manifestation of the creative impulse of the human consciousness. It is the realization and development in the environment of the Afro-American and the contact he has made with other groups. Mechanically, jazz is the art of drawing upon the intuitive man in a production of positive and negative musical elements. Positive and negative musical elements should be significant in any effective jazz archival program. As a jazz musician, I think that archives have been devoted to jazz history. They have not treated the concurrent problems of jazz musicians and the evolution of aesthetic continuum in jazz as part of the maturation of music in the United States.

Positive musical elements are those musical idiosyncracies that are projected from the inner nature of the musician. The negative elements can be seen as musical ideas which are external to the musical heritage of the musician, or the progenitors. Of course, when we say progenitors, we're talking about Japanese, Englishmen, the whole thing. When we recognize that the Afro-American musical idiom has permeated all the cultures of the civilized world, then we can recognize the great potential that universities, archives, and humanitarian forces have for bringing about rapport, harmony, and a new cultural phenomenon among the diverse cultures of the planet.

In a narrower sense, jazz is the art of the Afro-American as an expression of those universal principles governing artistic expression among the various races on earth. Various groups seem to respond to melody and rhythm differently. For example, French, Japanese, Italian, and Afro-American music are easily recognized. In each case, the same fundamental laws of sound are utilized, but the responses are different. Musically and philosophically, jazz is the integration of ideals and elements of African and European art.

As James Baldwin sees the African tradition, its art directly affects the lives of the people: whereas in European art, one has to be a part of a minority to derive benefit from it. The musical phenomenon we call jazz is characterized by its effect on the mass of the people, yet it is an evolved minority that is attuned to its effects. To me, as a jazz musician and an educator, this is significant in providing for the aesthetic continuum in its relevance to the development of diversity and maturity of music in American life.

Because of jazz's origin as a utilitarian art, problems have arisen since the old jazz masters evolved the art. When a Negro musician existed in sociological conditions that limited his media of expression to labor, entertainment, or some form of rebellion, jazz fulfilled the need for expression for the artist and entertainment for the people. In New Orleans, the accepted birthplace of jazz, musicians played for a livelihood, enjoyed identification with the useful segment of the community, and fulfilled their need for artistic expression.

As years passed, businessmen began exploiting jazz as a commodity. Later the record industry was born and it and players migrated for economic progress and jazz became more markedly involved with being. The time came when the jazz musician could no longer satisfy his need for inner expression and fulfill the idea of mass entertainment. As American society evolved, jazz became a steppingstone for a higher consciousness of the jazz musician. His music became more directly related to his sensitivity and response to his inner self.

I think that in America today we are at the stage in the metamorphic development of the jazz musician when he is involved with the aesthetic continuum on the vital, creative level in jazz. We have a new consciousness. We need and are pursuing things like Afro-American studies, black studies, and jazz archives. I think archives should assist universities and constructive forces in the United States to move Afro-Americans into the mainstream of

American life. This should be done by gearing archives to the totality of problems in jazz.

First, archives should deal with the preservation of jazz history. But they should also be dynamic, innovative, and aggressive, and channel the research and materials into facilities or environments that develop students of jazz.

At Southern University we are going to have courses in jazz improvisation, jazz history, jazz ensemble, jazz arranging, the business of music, and jazz media and theater. It would be wonderful if we could instantaneously draw from archival materials. We are fortunate in having the Archives of Jazz in New Orleans, but that is 80 miles away. What is needed is cooperative programs with educators and other people who have jazz programs.

It strikes me as odd that the admitted musical offering of America has only had a token of the resources of its culture at its disposal. Jazz has had to survive in an off-beat fashion and, to this day, its evolution has been dwarfed in spite of its ever-flowing spirit. I think this is significant because, although we can say that jazz has been developing, that it is wonderful, that it is the unique American contribution, we must also acknowledge a dissipation of aesthetic potential in wasted talent. Charlie Parker died at 35; Bix Beiderbecke had his career cut short; these phenomena have social and economic significance and far-reaching aesthetic implications.

I think that with the minds we have we can create a kind of coordinating network of archives, universities, and organizations dedicated to jazz preservation and development, and musicians themselves.

If such a cooperative effort were initiated, the jazz musician could indulge in some creative, innovative work which would also be of value to the archive. For instance, John Coltrane, at one time, was working with modes and rhythms. At his death he was working with new forms and had reached a new level of virtuosity on the saxophone. He did this although it was potential economic suicide and drew a very limited audience.

Jazz archives should be devoted to this kind of preservation because jazz has evolved to the point where musicians should be able to create some music free of economic pressures. At Southern University we are going to foster as much of this as our resources permit.

This does not mean that we reject traditionalists; this does not mean that we exclude; this does not mean that we just listen to Pharoah Sanders. It means that we treat, investigate, research, create opportunities for experimentation and experience for all kinds of music that relate to the entire spectrum of jazz. There is room for great diversity: for the student who becomes a rock-and-roll musician, the traditional player who preserves the old style, and the musician who uses instrumentation and techniques of composition supposedly outside of jazz to develop a new idiom.

Southern University has branches in New Orleans, Baton Rouge, and Shreveport. We are going to try to work with the Archive of New Orleans Jazz and the professional musicians in New Orleans to bring about a coalition between these facets of the music community. We hope that, eventually, we will have some kind of archival network to use in our work.

DEFINITIVE DISCOGRAPHY

Walter C. Allen
Discographer and Professor
Rutgers University

My interest is discography and the description of musicians' careers, particularly those of the older generation. I believe that the documentation of the recordings and the musical biography of a musician cannot be separated; his discography is a product of a man's career as much as anything else. I am going to discuss what the ideal archive would contain for a discographer like myself.

Preparing a discography involves three processes which often occur concurrently: gathering, organizing, and evaluating the material. An ideal jazz archive should offer not only as much data as possible, but they should be organized and indexed for maximum use.

The ideal archive should contain the complete periodical literature of jazz as well as the books, reference works, standard discographies such as Rust, Delaunay, and so forth. Such an ideal collection of the periodicals does not exist. The present periodical collection is badly organized and, with few exceptions, is not indexed.

For instance, a discographer might be studying James P. Johnson, born right here in New Brunswick, a pioneer figure who taught Fats Waller, and a brilliant stride pianist who wrote many standard jazz compositions and Broadway and touring shows. He is an important figure who has never really been documented.

To describe his career one would first search the literature, as academicians would say. Having gone through the existing discographies, which are at least somewhat indexed, one finds, first of all, that there are several James Johnsons; it is not an uncommon name. Lonnie Johnson, the folk blues guitarist, had a brother named James who played on some of his early records. Then there was James "Stump" Johnson. There are at least three piano players and some other instrumentalists named James Johnson. That is the first problem.

Another difficulty is that periodicals are not usually indexed. One thing the ideal archive would contain would be a "name concordance," if you will, of *Downbeat Magazine*. For all its defects, *Downbeat* is the primary surviving documentation of the period from 1934 onward.

Poets have concordances in which, literally, every word of the works of Shakespeare or Shelley is indexed as to the work, line, and paragraph from which it is extracted. A concordance of *names* of musicians would be a valuable tool and should be in the ideal jazz archive.

Almost every issue of *Downbeat* contains some reference to Louis Armstrong and there would be thousands of entries for him. There would not be as many for James P. Johnson, but tracing and searching the literature for him would be vastly simplified. At present, a researcher has to go, literally, through every available issue line by line. He cannot rely upon the titles of the major articles. When I worked on King Oliver, I found Oliver material in biographies of Albert Nicholas, Omer Simeon, Kid Ory, Armstrong, all kinds of people. A researcher must use his imagination and look in all kinds of unlikely places.

Of course, in all of this, the problem of preservation exists. For instance, no one knows if a complete set of *Downbeat* exists. I know it existed 20 years ago at the New York Public Library because I went through it, but last spring I requested the 1934-35-36 editions and found nothing left of 1934. There were only a few yellowed, half or one-quarter pages from 1935 entirely crumbled, and a few odd pages from 1936. These should be microfilmed before it is too late. Private collections should be sought and copied for the ideal archive.

Relevant pages from Negro newspapers, specifically as sources for playing and discographical information, should be on microfilm in the ideal archives. They are invaluable, with tremendous amounts and varieties of material.

Another source of information is the musician himself. Anyone who has talked to musicians about long-past recording sessions knows that there is a good chance of getting different recollections of a given performance. This is one area in which judgment is important. Eventually the material has to be evaluated and the records themselves become invaluable.

The researcher has to study the known recordings of James P. Johnson, those with his name on the label, for example, and learn to know what his style sounds like on wax. He made piano rolls, which are records, so these are compared with the discs. The ideal archive would have a complete collection of his sheet music and show scores. They should be played and compared with the recordings and the piano rolls. How do they differ? How are they alike? How much did he improvise? Did he follow the score? These are questions which certainly would go into the complete study of James P. Johnson.

I have mentioned that he taught Fats Waller. How is Fats similar? How does Fats differ from James P. in his piano? You would have to know what Fats sounded like, as well as Willie "the Lion." You would have to know what any of his other progenitors or pupils sounded like and be able to distinguish among them. This involves a lot of aural study. You have to develop a memory for the sound of James P. Johnson, so that when you hear it on a record, although his name is not on the label, you know that it is James P., not Fats. This is part of the evaluation.

Many reports will come from young and enthusiastic collectors identifying James P. on a given record. Then you have to search out the record, listen to it, and decide for yourself.

If there is documentary evidence, such as a contemporary news account of his recording at that time, you should know about it and document it. Therefore, the ideal archive should have all the recordings available, or a bank of information to help locate them in other archives or in private collections. Older collectors now know who most of the prominent collectors are and contact them when starting a project like this. Tapes are an ideal method of avoiding the risks of mailing records. Collectors often willingly tape a copy for fair use.

The ideal archive would also contain things like recording company ledgers of matrix number in numerical order. For sessions after about 1950, or the advent of the LP, the matrix number is of little importance; but in the days of the 78, the matrix number pressed into the record placed it in some sort of chronology in relation to other recordings. For example, three recordings with matrix numbers 1144, 1145, and 1146, all by the same band, were recorded together, probably on the same occasion. With the ledger, one could search out 1143 and 1147 to see whether these also include the musician being studied.

Interviews with musicians are excellent resources. Those of James P. Johnson's generation are, unfortunately, fast disappearing. The ideal archive would have taped interviews with as many people like Willie "the Lion" and Willie Gant, as possible. Fats, of course, is gone, but there are many other New York stride pianists like Beetle and Jack "the Bear" who should be located, if they are still alive, and interviewed on tape.

An additional source for researchers is photographs, both stills and movies. A sound moving picture is a recording just as much as a disc or a piano roll and has a visual record too. Ernie Smith mentioned James P. appearing in the film, "Emperor Jones." Perhaps he made others that would turn up in a search of film archives. An ideal film archive, as described by Fred Ramsey, would be an enormously useful research tool.

Occasionally, all the details you get jibe. For instance, during my work on King Oliver, I found that he made two sides with the vaudeville team of Butterbeans and Susie. These were recorded in New York at a time when he was regularly playing in Chicago, and, though his name was on the record label, labels have been wrong before. Was it possible that it really was he or was it somebody else?

When I talked to Clarence Williams, he casually mentioned that Joe had come to New York for a few days to try to get some engagements here and that he and Clarence went to the Harry Wills-Luis "Angel" Firpo fight. I wrote to *Ring Magazine* and got the date — September 1924, exactly the period during which the OKeh records with Butterbeans and Susie were made. This is powerful circumstantial evidence that he was in New York at the time, and that the label identification was correct. Occasionally, things check out beautifully; all sources mesh; you get to interview five musicians and they all have the same recollections of the date; you have newspaper accounts, and you have other evidence. Occasionally this happens, but not often.

As you follow up these leads, each seems to generate others until, hopefully, there seems a natural, appropriate place to stop. Having gathered the information and, of tremendous importance, documenting it accurately, you must organize it. This should be done in such a way that maximum use can be made of the data, reorganizing them if necessary.

Finally, the data must be evaluated, especially for accuracy. Though, as I have noted, some evaluations are made while the data are being gathered, an overall evaluation of the work must be made at the conclusion of the research.

An ideal archive would facilitate and encourage jazz research and preservation.

JAZZ, EDUCATION, AND THE COMMUNITY

Christopher W. White
Department of Music, Rutgers — Newark
Jazz Musician and Executive Director
Summer on Wheels Inc.

I work with Summer On Wheels, an organization operating in New York State under a contract with the New York State Council on the Arts. We are involved in all of the arts as producers, advisors, agents, and managers. Our primary objective is to raise the level of existence for artists by using new methods and approaches.

Currently, we have two projects under way: street, or mobile, theater and community workshops in the arts. In addition to its bringing theater into small communities and neighborhoods and providing jobs and training for artists and performers, mobile theater is a lever for getting into the community to establish workshops. Also, funding agencies relate to mobile theater as a means of community pacification.

Of course, mobile theater has existed for centuries in Europe, but here it is enjoying a renaissance, and we have been fortunate in being involved in its revival in New York from the very beginning. My interest grew out of working with Jazzmobile in 1967. Since then at least 25 mobile theater companies which are self-sufficient in terms of lights, sound systems, generators, etc., have developed in New York.

They are able to go into a block and, within a period of 10 minutes to an hour, start their performance. Of course, there is a lot of preparation and community relations work done prior to the performance; that is what we do for the groups. The tenor of the times is such that neighborhoods must be prepared before anybody rolls in or you may get Molotov Cocktails all over your float. We arouse interest and gain access to the community through the theater.

We are currently operating in 26 cities throughout New York State and are pretty much aware of who's doing what and where in the whole spectrum of the arts — dance; theatre; and music, both jazz and other idioms. While establishing community relations for the performances, we also find out what kind of a workshop would go best in the community. Our workshops are places where someone can receive free, professional instruction in any art form.

If we organize a jazz community workshop, it would, ideally, be run by a musician from that community. We would try to find a musician working in that area who would be capable of running a workshop encompassing all areas of jazz music and instructions. Hopefully, enough money would be available to give him two or three part-time assistants. This would free him from fund raising and administrative duties.

The workshops are havens for professional musicians, as teachers, administrators, and traveling consultants. Hopefully, they would get good fees for their services and a chance to develop creatively, free of the pressures of making a living.

I would now like to describe a specific workshop that I designed before I joined Summer On Wheels and discuss how it relates to archives. It is administered by Rhythm Associates, a unique organization which I run, and which was founded by part of the Dizzy Gillespie rhythm section. We started by operating rhythm section seminars for professional musicians who had, technically, mastered their instruments. However, it has evolved differently.

The school is run by a faculty of professional musicians who make their living as jazz players and whose survival depends on how proficient they are. Since they are surviving, we assume that their approach and method are acceptable today — that is what we are interested in. Because there are so many approaches to playing, all of which are acceptable, we wanted to find and offer a collective approach to the serious student. We wanted to find out how each individual musician developed his own style. It was simple, once we got together our group of about 15 players.

After eliminating all the personal idiosyncrasies, a collective approach to developing a genuine style of improvisation breaks down into three steps. First, develop as an instrumentalist. There is no shortcut — particularly if you are going to succeed today. You are not going to make a living playing jazz in some nice honkytonk. To survive you have to be a versatile and proficient musician. Secondly, train your ear, and finally, listen to and analyze as many jazz improvisations as possible. By exposing yourself to different styles you will, hopefully, find a person or persons with whom you have some sort of stylistic sympathy.

To develop technical, vocal, or instrumental ability, the first of the three steps outlined above, we have devised methods to introduce the student to the jazz idiom immediately. While he is learning how his instrument works, instead of throwing the usual method book in front of him, we use special materials written by the school's faculty. This material uses jazz rhythms, harmonies, and melodies and, at the same time, prepares the student technically.

In developing the ear we do the same thing. We use phonograph records a great deal for students to transcribe or write down music from recordings. This is done slowly at first, but as he progresses the student is encouraged to work faster. This approach is similar to what most music schools call a dictation course.

Finally, encouraging the development of style is an intriguing portion of what we do, and is the area in which the community-based educational program is most relevant to the archives.

Rhythm Associates received a grant from the Brooklyn Institute of Arts and Sciences to run a jazz workshop at a place called Muse, in Bedford-Stuyvesant. (It was an old car showroom that a fine architect redesigned into a really groovy-looking place.) When we got into this community workshop we found that this three-step approach worked because it was a logical way to approach developing a style of improvisation in jazz.

The third step is the hardest. Many people think that you can't teach anyone how to play jazz. What they mean is that it is difficult to give direction. It is a very personal thing, because once you learn what notes are in a chord, how to play them, and the various rhythms involved — syncopation and so forth — it is hard to teach how to interpret feeling. The only way to get the student on that road is to expose him to as many improvisors as possible, let him decide what person is closest to his improvisational style, and then use that person's style as a point of departure.

When he listens to this musician we do not want him to merely listen and learn by rote. We want him to be analytical about the musician's approach and start to understand how he used a combination of notes in relation to the rhythm section, or how the harmony of that particular combination conveyed a certain feeling. We found that once a person has been drawn to a stylistic approach and is taught to analyze it his way his ability to improvise grows.

At our workshop we have limited access to records. An archive would help us immensely if records were catalogued so that they were readily available, and if various individual musicians' solos were collected on tapes to represent their stylistic family tree. Let us consider John Coltrane as an example. Where does John Coltrane come from? Who are the influences that he incorporated into his style? Two would be Sonny Stitt and Charlie Parker, but we would have to go back further to Sidney Bechet. That work should be done carefully by qualified musicians and historians.

At the stage when a musician has developed his technical ability then he is his own teacher. He is a self-motivating, self-directing individual who does not have the time to collect and compile, but does need this kind of stylistic data. Since the archive exists and the recordings needed to do the stylistic tree exist, the student should have access to them. I believe that the archive makes no contribution to community education or to promoting interest in becoming a jazz musician if the records are not available.

I have developed a stylistic family tree for the bass. I would listen to a record, tape off a Ray Brown solo; an excerpt from, maybe, an Ellington with Blanton. Listening to solos in that order you start to see how styles develop and are related. This is what should be done to make archives relevant. This is what should be done to make archives relevant to the musician. This stylistic approach should also be applied to arranging and composing.

There is a gentleman in Philadelphia who has a doctorate in sociology and teaches at Fisk University. He has a phenomenal ear, and has developed a computerized stylistic tree system. I met him at a club in Philadelphia where he would transcribe people's solos, not note for note, but analytically, and trace them back to the tree. He has worked out a way of programming these data into a computer and having the stylistic trees available and cross-referenced in 30 seconds. People like this should be employed so that all the material is available and useful to the musician who is attempting to find direction as an improvisor.

Another function of the archives, especially those affiliated with institutions like a university, is outreach. It is great to have an archive, but if nobody knows of its existence, it is useless. I did not know Rutgers had the Marshall Stearns collection until about 1968. I am in the jazz field and feel that I am pretty much on top of things, but I did not hear about it.

You have to remember that the music that we are talking about came from the community; you cannot isolate it and make it so esoteric that you dehumanize it. Jazz came from the community and it should be available to the community. If anyone says archives are really not open, that they are really for research, that is hogwash. If that is what you are about, it sounds very much like separatism to me.

PRESERVATION AND EXTENSION OF THE JAZZ HERITAGE

Summary of two panel discussions

Discussion among the panelists and members of the audience developed the following major points:

First, there is a pressing need to promote an interchange of persons and information among the various important sound collections, like those at Lincoln Center, Rutgers, Tulane, and Stanford.

Second, such archives should cooperate with private collectors, who often can rival any archive in one or two highly specialized areas. Such cooperation will preserve permanently the strengths of such private collections and thereby make them more widely available than the private owner can do.

Third, the question of taping collections — private or institutional — raises complex legal questions on which the law itself is vague and test cases are lacking.

Institutions can apparently receive any materials for listening on the premises without legal risks, providing they permit no indiscriminate copying. There is a basic distinction, even for listening, between a reference library serving researchers and a circulating library serving the general public. No single library can serve both clienteles; all research-oriented libraries, university-based or not, restrict listening privileges to qualified persons making specialized use of the materials.

The legal aspects of duplicating materials on tape are not clear. The problem is not really one of copyright law but of proprietary rights. Institutions are fearful of legal problems, especially of lawsuits brought by recording companies. Some observers feel this fear is groundless; no suits have occurred, and commercial firms may hesitate to sue a non-profit library or university. Nevertheless, institutions will remain timid pending some ground rules clearly defining the concept of "fair use." Not now clearly embodied in copyright law, such a definition might be developed between the recording industry and the Association for Recorded Sound Collections. Another body concerned with the problem, and a source of information on it, is the Council on Library Resources in Washington.

Fourth, another area of legal concern is the question of taping live performances. Performers object strenuously, because they receive no additional compensation for the recording which takes place and because such recording weakens the demand for their commercial recordings. They feel strongly that the audience is paying for enjoyment of the particular live performance and not the right to repeat it, via tape, in perpetuity.

Concert halls and theaters attempt to prevent such taping, but it takes place constantly (although almost always with limitations of equipment and placement which preclude the use of the tapes for commercial reproduction). A person who attempted to sell his tape of a live performance might be courting legal trouble, but he is most unlikely to have any trouble if the tape is restricted to his private use. Nevertheless, some unauthorized tapes have resulted in bootleg records, which sell under the counter in some New York stores. An archive could acquire such a record or tape with impunity, but should never circulate it.

The musicians' union is also involved, seeking to protect the interests of performers in general and sidemen in particular; the leader of a performance may acquiesce in a taping without the permission of the sidemen or any compensation to them.

Fifth, it is vital to extend the riches of a jazz archive to a wide public, despite the many problems involved. A few archives have a very limited capability to enable people to study the development of a style or performer; with sufficient advance notice, they may produce a tape for on-premises listening. But such facilities are rare and relatively primitive. All archives lack adequate staff to respond to such requests, even with advance notice, because of the considerable time involved in locating materials and taping them. Archives are chronically starved for funds and under pressure to limit their staffs and working hours.

One possible form of service would be to prepare printed materials on key jazz performers. The person interested in a given performer usually lacks the time, musical training, and/or discographical expertise to identify the key recordings, but he might put together his own tape for study if he had a printed guide and access to the recordings in the archive. However, this requires supervision, as well as the preliminary creation of a usable catalogue and the printed guides to key performers.

Sixth, part of the problem of extending the archival resources lies in the identification of the many "publics" to be served. Several universities, including Rutgers, seek to create outreach programs involving jazz in the community and in the schools. The archival resources can be used to prepare teaching materials on various levels for the schools, probably stressing historical development and the appreciation of the major styles and figures, and more advanced materials for young musicians aspiring to become professionals. Discographers and other scholars make still other demands on an archive, usually requiring direct contact with the materials. Perhaps most challenging is the need to achieve ultimate service to the general public, which wants an opportunity to hear a wide range of the music but may not require full access to the archive itself.